Colours of a Rainbow

PATRICK CLIFFORD

Colours of a Rainbow
Copyright©2023 Patrick Clifford
ALL RIGHTS RESERVED.
Including the right of reproduction in whole or in part in any form.
International copyright secured.
ISBN: 978-1-914488-92-4
This edition printed and bound in the Republic of Ireland by

lettertec

Lettertec Ireland Ltd
Springhill House,
Carrigtwohill
Co. Cork
Republic of Ireland
www.selfpublishbooks.ie

No part of this publication may be reproduced or transmitted by any device, without the prior written permission of the copyright holder.
This book may not be circulated without a cover or in any cover other than the existing cover.

Contents

A Memoir 1
    Colours of a Rainbow 1

Poems 7
    Colours of a Rainbow 7
    The Afterlife 13
    I Promise 16
    Broaden Your Horizons 19
    Cheer Up 21
    Internal Affairs 25
    Fairies In the Tree 28
    Loss of Identity 30
    Obsession 33
    Life's Choices 36
    Born A Slave 40
    The Real World 43
    Fatal Aggression 48
    Eternal Flame 51
    A Bottomless Pit 55
    Urban Uprising 59
    Calming the Storm 64
    Crocodile Tears 67
    Seek The Rainbow's End 70
    Symphony of A Rag Town 74

The Bottle 78
Awakening of a Wake 81

Haiku 83

Limericks 89

Songs 93

Hello Darling 93
A Never-Ending Show 96
A Starlit Night.. 99
A Rainbow's End 103
Dear Norah 107
Old-School 111
Voices in Our Heart... 115
The Road Home... 118
Growing Older 122
Warmth of an Angel 126
Alone and Lonely...130
Little Bird..135
Kings On a Throne...139
Summertime...143
Lazy Days 147
Rasta Rasta Rainbow....................................... 151
Troubled Times 155
Mama Don't Go 159
Rise of the Underdog.......................................163
The Cuckoo's Nest 167

Hometown 171
  Masters 175
  Players 179
  Crossing Over 183
  Wild Horses 187
  A Gift 192
  Soulmate 196
  You're a Ghost 200
  Oh Shari 205
  Christmas Of Joy and Peace 208
  A Jolly Christmas Time 212
  A Little Red Robin 216

Rap Poetry 221
  Aristocrats 221
  Ghost Train 225
  Streetwise 230
  A Dark Cloud Appears 235
  An Alleyway to Paradise 239
  Higher Power 243

Acknowledgements

I would like to thank Hail for helping me to publish this book, for their support, influence and guidance.

Also, to Bluebird and recovery groups
for their inspiration.

To my friends and family for their
support and encouragement.

Thank you for the opportunity to publish this book.

A Memoir
Colours of a Rainbow

Growing up in the suburbs of Dublin as a young boy in the 1970's and 1980's was a totally different time and place than it is now.

I came from a medium sized family of my two parents and my three sisters. The areas where I grew up was Dublin 12 Walkinstown, Drimnagh, and Crumlin.

Both my parents worked and had good jobs we always had meals and clothes and went to Wexford every summer on holidays and sometimes to Mosney.

I could not communicate properly as a young kid at home, with friends, playing football, in school, and suffered with anxiety, shame and low self-esteem.

I could not concentrate in school lessons. I was clever enough but through getting into fights, daydreaming, being bullied I started to mitch from school at an early age of 8 years old.

The one thing I liked in school was the football as I was not a bad player, and I was quite skilful but again I did not think I was any good.

I started getting into trouble as a kid especially when my father passed away from a massive heart attack. I was eleven years old, and I missed him so much I could not cope and started to drink and smoke cannabis for the ease and comfort take the edge off the emotional pain.

By the age of twelve I had dropped out of secondary school. Halfway into my first year I had got expelled over a fight. They were going to give me a second chance, but I decided not to go back.

At the age of fifteen I was depending on alcohol and drugs as I was drifting out of a normal life in full flight from reality. I was dating girls and at fifteen I got into a relationship with a girl. Two years into the relationship we had a son: I was only seventeen, she was eighteen.

I had no job or income. I was getting into trouble with the police and was homeless on and off the streets from the age of fourteen.

When my son was two years old my partner and I split up and went our separate ways. I was living on the streets in doorways, park benches, homeless hostels. I ended up on remand in St Patrick's institution, then transferred to Dundrum Central Mental and then to St Loman's hospital where I was diagnosed with drug induced psychosis at eighteen.

Eventually I realised after drinking there for four years that I had to try and stop so I went to recovery at the age of twenty-four. I was slowly being rehabilitated.

My mental and physical condition had improved as I was going to meetings and to the gym.

I was in hospital just waiting to get sorted with accommodation as I was doing well. I was crossing the motorway and I was knocked down as a pedestrian. I was pronounced dead at the scene. A doctor who was passing by resuscitated me and I was rushed to hospital to ICU. I went into a coma and had to undergo surgery for thirty-eight hours on my pelvis which was crushed. I had to get forty units of blood pumped into me. I had broken ribs, punctured lung, broken left leg in four places, broken ankle, right footdrop, broken collar, and shoulder bones. I was in a coma for six weeks and life support for eight weeks.

They said in the ICU that I would never make it. One day I just woke up out of the coma in severe pain, not knowing what had happened but I was grateful. I could not communicate for a week or two. I was not sure if I would ever walk again as it took years of physio before I could walk without an aid or crutches. It was a struggle, but I got there in the end.

As my life resumed, I got into a high support hostel, then to a medium support hostel then to a low support hostel. Then for the first time ever I got my own home which I shared with another person. I then got my own apartment where I have lived for the last thirteen years.

In the last fifteen years I done a FETAC level two course in New Horizons where I started to write poetry. Then I done my junior cert, leaving cert, Threshold training course, creative writing class in Gateway Project, Diploma in Addiction Studies/Counselling in Liberties College. In the last five years I have written and published four books and I am in the process of publishing book number five. I also perform and record some of my songs in studio, open mics and events/gigs.

Six years ago, I was diagnosed with Parkinson's disease unfortunately for me the disease has progressed and some of the symptoms are starting to show: my movement, walking, speech, sleep pattern, weight gain have been affected and progressed worse.

In the last three years I have nearly died with double pneumonia and then with Covid-19 as my immune system is low because of my underlying condition. I mostly use a mobility scooter to get around or a rollator for support.

I am currently working as a peer support volunteer/worker with Hail Housing. I co-manage a football team, Hail United, organising football games, tournaments, and training drills and sessions. I also help run the Hail Music Group which we recently recorded two songs, one of the songs 'Set Sail' I wrote the lyrics to. Hail have also awarded me a bursary grant to help with my new book and I am grateful to them for that.

I am twenty-six years sober and clean, never forgetting all the near-death experiences and places where I ended up, situations I found myself in, and the ailments and diagnosis I have been diagnosed with. I need to keep on going forward and try accepting things that happen in my life good and bad. That I need to look after myself more so now than I ever did. My home help, Bluebird Care, has also been great help and support to me.

My family have been a great support to me as they try and look after their own lives, they still help me if I need them - my mother and my sisters, thanks to them for that.

The reason I wrote this memoir solely about a reflection of some of my life was to do with the colours of the rainbow. The rainbow in the sky baffled me like a mystique and magic. I was always trying to find the rainbow's end. Some of the folklore, stories, movies, it's just magical and warming to see the colours of a rainbow. In my darkest, loneliest days, hours, even minutes has saved me from a darker shade into the light.

When I had no hope and needed a friend,
I sought the curiosity of a rainbows end.
There is only one place you have left to go,
It is the magic and healing of the colours of a rainbow.

Poems

Colours of a Rainbow

Sometimes when the sun shines
And it's raining,
Somewhere at the same time,
A rainbow may appear.

This is how I feel when it's grey and dull
Of my heart and spirit,
As the colours of a rainbow,
Changes the atmosphere.

Each one of the seven
Colours of the rainbow
Represents good feelings
That are special to me.

It's a sense of bewilderment
One gets from this.
A magical, mystical work of
Nature in all its entirety.

I am relating the
First colour in the rainbow.
When I' am struggling
To make it out of bed.

This symbolises the
Blood in my veins, what
Keeps my heart beating.
I relate to the colour red.

The second colour is orange,
Which represents
To me when I'm broken
Down and don't tick a box.

When I am envious to be in control,
Eloquent, intelligent, and sophisticated.
Orange represents the beauty and
Cleverness of a vixen, female fox.

The third colour is yellow,
Which precipitates me when I can't
Stand up for myself because of my
Traumatic experience when' I'm full of fear.

Yellow you're like a heroine, wearing a
Bright armoured suit, lighting the darkness.
Even in my worst nightmare you give me
Strength helping me face another year.

The fourth colour is green.
Sometimes I feel lost, bewildered and
Like I'm on another planet
At the end of a movie scene.

Green shows me a path to freedom
And to what's real in my life,
Giving me gratitude as I walk along
Sandy beaches or lay in a field of green.

The fifth colour is blue which is traditionally
A boy's colour, a symbol of machoism.
The social rules blue, is restricting its labels,
And stops me falling in love.

Blue is serene and walks and talks like an angel
Letting me into the Book of Love,
I feel the freshness of Spring again, with blue,
Dreams from above.

The sixth colour is indigo, an intriguing colour
Of purple, reminding me of slavery,
Gives me the essence of lavender,
I hold like blooming flower.

I was a slave to misery and hypocrisy,
Which Indigo was representable?
As the colour indigo came to me
Which restored my faith in a higher power?

The seventh colour is violet which is
A captivating colour of calmness.
This is rounding off the seven colours,
Rainbow soothing my soul.

Never forget the entertainment or
Colour, zest and happiness, that
The rainbow has brought to children.
This mysterious rainbow has taken control.

Rivers of dreams flow
To the end of the rainbow.
Magic that lights the sky, without it
To reach the end we would die.

Beauty is a mysterious craft,
One look you laugh.
Somewhere, someday,
Beyond the rainbow,
We will fly away.
These colours of the rainbow,
We will never let them go.
Colours of a rainbow.
Colours of a rainbow.

Described as a spinning wheel
Of energy there are seven main chakras
Running along the spine.
What is the rainbow bridge?
When all the chakras are open
Energy can run through them
Freely and harmony exists
Between the physical body, mind, and spirit.
The seven chakras:
1 The root chakra. 2 The sacral chakra.
3 The solar plexus chakra. 4 The throat chakra.
5 The heart chakra. 6 The third eye chakra.
7 The crown chakra.

Definition of spiritual awakening is to become aware of
Your surroundings to be awoken or reborn.

The Afterlife

As the clock ticks and
The World spins round,
Is there an afterlife? And
Where can it be found?

In our lives like the
Change of season,
Like a wandering star,
That has no reason.

Who has courage,
Who has faith
To reach a destination,
Of miracles that create?

On our death bed,
We must be brave,
To go to a better
Place beyond the grave.

Repenting is not like we
Believe in reincarnation.
Those who have no rights,
And are dying of starvation.

If we believe in ourselves,
We indeed may come back.
Even if we spent our lives
On a runaway track.

Is there a magical Kingdom?|
Or a heaven above?
To a futuristic galaxy,
We may experience new love.

If we keep it simple
Until our dying day.
Entering a spiritual entity,
far beyond the milky way.

Like a flower in bloom,
We are reborn from
A life of treachery,
So twisted and torn.

Into the Earth's soil,
As we get lowered under,
We hope to avoid fire,
Brimstone and thunder.

No one has ever come back
To give us an insight
Of the afterlife, be
It darkness or light.

Can we see the afterlife?
In our new-born baby's cry?
Or taste eternal freedom,
Somewhere beyond the sky?

Were all on different paths
Through our pain and strife.
Our destination
Is to reach the afterlife.

The afterlife, the afterlife,
The afterlife.

I Promise

Looking back through the years,
Common denominator was my fears.
I could never tell people I felt weak,
The hero inside I could never seek.

I promise I will not badly behave,
To iniquities and anxiety, I am a slave.
I promise I will get things done,
Being alive is about having fun.

Life is like a stage,
As I turn another page.
Help me to get through,
Sometimes I don't have a clue.

I promise you this,
True love in my kiss.
I promise you much more,
If you will walk through my door.

I cannot promise you wealth and fame,
I will always try play my winning game.
I promise you realistic hopes and dreams,
No more lies and money-making schemes.

I promise, I promise,
No more Doubting Thomas.
I promise, I promise, I promise.
Precession and homage.

I promise I will be honest when I am wrong,
I will always sing your favourite love song.
I cannot promise the sun, moon, and stars,
I promise I will try and heal your wounded scars.

I promise, I will shine a light,
If the future is not looking bright.
I promise sheer bliss,
To guide you through the abyss.

I promise I will be your hammer and nail,
To hold you when you're old and frail.
I promise roses and wine,
Of a life so fulfilling and divine.

I promise, you breathe in the air,
I promise, I will always be there.
I promise, we'll to be together until the end.
I promise, to afar we will transcend.

I promise love forever more,
I promise you will know the score.
I promise I will be your clown,
Cheer you up when you're feeling down.

I promise, you my truth,
I promise you will get my sleuth,
I promise, I promise, I promise,
I promise, I promise.

Broaden Your Horizons

As the clock ticks twenty-four hours,

Nature's beauty of sunshine and showers,

Drinking a coffee, you feel like you're
up in the clouds,

Broaden your horizons by mingling in
with the crowds.

In this life you only get back of what you give,

As dreams of success in your mind start to relive.

Aim high and focus on being in a positive direction,

A total transformation of character
is like a resurrection.

Broaden your horizons as life may one
day pass you by,

A sense of achievement has brought a
twinkle to your eye.

Iniquities and complications you hope
will be banished,

From your old internal jail, you seen a

light and vanished.

When the smearing smog comes to remind
you of your darkened past,

You will send it into the sea of forgetfulness
with a blast.

Broaden your horizons and keep going,

It will happen automatically without you knowing.

Broaden your horizons until your dying day,

For it's what you do not what you say.

Broaden your horizons,

Of colour and zest,

To be yourself is to be your best.

Broaden your horizon.

Broaden your horizon.

Cheer Up

Cheer up why
You look so sad.
Memories and feelings,
Is all you ever had.

Lift your head up,
From off the ground.
Cheer up, cheer up,
You will be safe and sound.

Follow your gut instinct,
Wherever you may go.
As your heart keeps you,
Warm in the cold and snow.

Think of positive and
Good vibrations
As you're carrying a negative
Crutch of previous generations.

Get off the cross because
We may need the wood.
Giving yourself a tough time
Can be misunderstood.

Think of someone else,
Who is in a darker place?
Cheer up, cheer up
With a warm embrace.

You maybe all alone
With no one to love.
Laughing at yourself is a
touch from an angel above.

All you may need,
Is shelter and food.
Cheer up my friend,
Life can be so shroud.

Happiness can come
Like a telegraph.
You're so funny,
Give me your autograph.

Dry your eyes mate
As you make my sun shine.
Broken hearts,
Are well in decline.

Cheer up, cheer up,
You will never reach the top.
Just keep on climbing,
As life will never ever stop.

Cool as cucumber,
And top of the pile.
Cheer up, cheer up,
Live life for a while.

Cheer up, my buddy,
Cheer up, my friend.
One fine day we will
Meet at the rainbow's end.

Cheer up, cheer up,
It's never too bad.
For the gift of life,
We all should be glad.

Cheer up, cheer up,
Cheer up.

C – Charisma
H – Humility,
E – Education,
E – Experience,
R – Respect,
U – Unity,
P – Perseverance.

Internal Affairs

Reflecting inwardly on
Life's on-going despairs.
Inner investigations of
Your internal affairs.

Looking from the inside
Like the change of seasons.
Through stormiest weather
We search for honest reasons.

The sun will shine brightly,
But only from the sky.
Feel your emotions and
Do not be ashamed to cry.

Sentimental values you
Have for your true love
Are almost non-existent
As the push comes to shove.

Find a way to a higher power,
Clean the debris from your past,
Observations of self-honesty is,
Healing and leaves you feeling aghast.

Like a disease or a disorder that,
Centres in your unconscious mind.
Healing of internal affairs is a
Perception untangling and entwined.

No need to carry the weight
Of the world upon your shoulder.
Enjoy life be happy, joyous and free
As you will gradually get frail and older.

Internal affairs are not a critic
Or a political legislation,
They can be disturbing thoughts,
Leaving you feeling demoralisation.

Sometimes you would not treat
Your worst enemy as you treat yourself.
Internal affairs can be clear thinking,
Just like cleaning and freshening the delft.

Who wants to be negative
And live in a sorrowful bubble.
Start looking at healing the inside,
As you could be heading for trouble.

Your mind is to be healthy depending
On its signals of a positive manifestation.
How you exhale and succeed in the World
May be prior to your honest examination.

To climb to the top of the stairs
You need to look at internal affairs.
To become spiritually aware's
Is to use a tool of internal affairs.
Internal affairs, internal affairs.

Fairies In the Tree

Sometimes things seem not real,

To see a fairy all sickness can heal.

As they capture our imagination

Of a fairy-tale that's prior to investigation.

In a magical forest Fairies live in a tree,

Just one look at them could set you free.

They chant in a language we don't understand,

Bringing the best out in us by spreading magical sand.

They fly so fast with their enchanting powers,

Brightening up our spirits like a bunch of flowers.

Fairies live in a tree: it's not a myth or folk-law.

I was at the other side because it was a fairy I saw.

With no expectations or feelings that are contrary,

We can never hurt or capture the myth of a fairy.

You can be happy and free,

Coz you see fairies, live in a tree.

Like butterflies along a stream,

Fairies take us from a nightmare to a dream.

You often hear fairies of being weak,

They are so powerful it is like to hide and seek.

I will never forget when I was set free,

I opened my eyes and seen fairies live in a tree.

Fairies live in a tree,

Of mystic and glee.

Fairies live in a tree,

Guiding you and me.

Not everyone can see,

That Fairies live in a tree.

Fairies live in a tree.

Loss of Identity

Like a falling leaf blowing
Amid the Autumn breeze.
Faith alone cannot tell me
If I am standing or on my knees.

Somewhere down the line my family
Have forgotten who we are.
Years of substance abuse like
Amnesia has taking us too far.

Looking at old photographs,
Reminiscing of my family tree,
Still cannot make head nor tails,
Of my truest self and identity.

Rummaging through the archives
Of my poor dark livelihood:
A small fish in a big pond,
Underdog that was misunderstood.

In my subconscious mind
I relieve a euphoric recall.
Blasted back in time louder
And faster than a cannonball.

For those I have loved,
Of whom I know in my heart,
Distant voices and memories,
Of a futile existence torn apart.

If only I could turn back time,
And straighten out my grief,
Writing a letter to my soul,
In the form of that fallen leaf.

If I could change my
Behaviour for each season,
To find my identity,
Would give me every reason.

Looking in the mirror I may,
Not know who is looking back.
From this hostility and loneliness,
I want to be myself and get on track.

I am who I am,
It is what it is.
I am not glum,
I am the biz.

I want to be me,
I do not want to be you.
To be myself is
Enough to see me through.

A distinct entity is a
Loss of my identity.
I shall go far
With my guiding star.

For the loss of my identity
I have peace and serenity.

Loss of identity,
Loss of identity.

Obsession

Inside my idle mind is a
High of another session.
Anticipating in fear and dread
The selfishness of an obsession.

It's a progressive illusion that
Like the moon is hard to break.
Swallowing my emotional pain,
Powerlessness over the intake.

The adrenaline in my mind
That craves that illusive high ...
Bowing down to addiction,
As the river slowly runs dry.

Can no one hear my cry for help
As I slowly drift into insanity.
It will be different next time,
The obsession is a form of vanity.

The obsession has me in denial
On the frontline in its trenches.
Occurrence of a physical allergy,
I cannot stop knowing the consequences.

This obsession will take away my life,
Leaving me all alone and out in the cold.
It has no respect of persons or sympathy,
Whatever gender, race, young, or old.

An obsession in its form can be anything,
Drugs, sex, alcohol, gambling, and food.
To get a fix for these obsessions is baffling,
It'll say I am doing well and lighten my mood.

No one wants to be deemed a failure,
An outcast from society and cast aside.
As the hole gets deeper, and deeper,
keeping me alive is a false sense of pride.

To treat an obsession that centres in my mind,
I need to have what's called a vital physic change,
To be set free from this fatal, progressive obsession,
So, my whole life and thinking can rearrange.

Obsession, obsession, I can
Stop its progression,
If I have a confession,
Is I have a mental obsession,
I give my concession,
That I have an obsession.
An obsession, obsession,
Obsession.

Life's Choices

In our youths
We have ambitions:
Prospects and prosperity,
Fear of foolish decisions.

As a young child
Attending school,
Low self-esteem,
We broke the rule.

Not knowing life is
Made by our choices,
Cannot live in reality
Of our broken voices.

Who wants to be normal,
And never get on a high,
Break the law for a living,
Listen to the angel's cry?

A judge will tell us,
We have been before,
Broken hearts and promises,
As the lock the prison door.

Getting back in the ring,
It will be different this time,
Lost the power of choice,
To ourselves is the worst crime.

Meeting a soul mate and
Falling madly in love.
Everything fitted perfect as
Bad choices loosened the glove ...

Fear of failure and success,
Who wants poverty or wealth?
Do we want to be sane and happy,
Or a grouch with poor mental health?

It's not possible for the world
To think and behave the same.
Our good and bad choices may decide,
if we will survive and stay in the game.

What if the whole world froze
And turned to solid stone.
If you were the last person alive,
Could you face life on your own.

We are not defined by our ailments,
Of how we think, act, and behave.
But we may be judged by our choices,
Which we may take beyond the grave.

How can we redeem ourselves and our
Choices make the world a better place.
It is progression not perfection if we have faith
And seek a solution, a good life we can embrace.

Life is life and the story goes on and on,
If you're not sure of something seek advice.
It might stop your world from crumbling by
Sharing it will help you make the right choice.

Life is like a cake,
We all want a slice.
To fulfil our ambitions
Is to try make the right choice.

Life's choices, life's choices,
Are like our own unique devices.
If our lives get tangled, we can try and splice,
To untangle we may need to make a choice.

Life's choices, Life's choices,
Are like occurring voices.
Life's choices,
Life's choices.

Born A Slave

Born a slave there
Is no second chance.
Tribes that worship the moon
Survive like they're in a trance.

Rituals and paganism may be
The only celebrated times
For peasants and farmers who
Are tortured for another man's crimes.

As the sun beams down on a land
Plagued by food and water drought.
Millions die of slavery and starvation,
No one to turn to as they scream and shout.

As we look in the mirror we are almost
Certain it's our reflection that is looking back.
Born a slave there is no identity in our past,
Or going forward there is no beating track.

What is the colour of our skin or our
Ethnic minority as society closes it door.
While charities and people try to help,
As slaves to addiction cry in the night for more.

A modern day of slavery is people fleeing
Countries from war, death and prostitution.
Asylum seekers that seek refuge on a boat,
To the insane locked up in an institution.

Every Country all around this World needs a,
Wakeup call for humanity to try and engage.
Or we will all stuck on the same old chapter,
At a standstill afraid to turn over to anew page.

Try not let the news get us unawares,
Or the betrayal of slavery gets us down.
It's been going on through our history,
There are too many Kings wearing one crown.

All we must do is look and walk,
In someone else's unfortunates' shoes,
So easy to fall into the poverty trap.
Or to be born a slave we just did not choose.

We must be brave,

When were born a slave.

Hurt me, hurt you,

You will do as they say you do.

Hard labour to stay alive

To have a number we may survive.

Toughness is something we might crave

To be born a slave is nothing more brave.

A letter of hope we send,

You will not be a slave but a friend.

Born a slave, born a slave.

Born a slave.

The Real World

Wake up, wake up,
From your sleep.
Count your blessings,
Not jumping sheep.

Sleep walking,
In a nightmare.
Nobody's home,
Coz nobody's there.

To get away from yourself
You need a constant high.
Escape the real World,
Kiss your emotions goodbye.

You have no responsibilities,
Living in an invisible bubble,
The more you drift from reality,
You could be heading for trouble.

What is all the fuss about?
What is the flipping point?
You just want to lie in bed
And smoke another joint.

I will meet you at the
Crossroads of a destination.
To reach the real world
Is a sweet sensation.

Big City lights is for
Those who are blind.
A way out of darkness,
They cannot find.

Listen to your heart
As it beats very fast.
On a train to nowhere,
Speeding from your past.

Get up, get up, get up
From your weary bed.
Do not listen to the
Negativity in your head.

You have travelled a long
Way alone in your room.
The real world can be fun,
Not full of doom and gloom.

One thing that's certain,
We're going to get older.
Why carry the world's
Weight upon your shoulder.

There is nothing more
Magical than a Rainbow.
Stand by the mystical river
And go with the elusive flow.

Hitch hike to infinity,
Or drift into outer space.
Not comfortable with, yourself
Everything will be hard to face.

The real world may not
Be like a Pleasure Dome.
Getting back from a journey,
It is home sweet home.

You do not need to be a genie,
Or have magical powers,
To be free from obsessions,
And our depressive, loneliest hours.

Sometimes all we need,
Is a trusted friend
To save us from anguish
And going round the bend.

It is so relaxing to
See a loving smile.
Take you from pain
For a little while.

If you're clean and
Tempted to go astray,
It's the real world that
Will direct you the right way.

Get off the fence,
Get off the wall,
Get off the bottom,
Do not need to crawl.

Keep it simple,
Keep it real.
This is life,
Not a deal.

The real World at
Times may be raw.
You opened your
Eyes and finally saw.

The real world, the real world,
The real world.

Fatal Aggression

As the passive people
Lay down to rest,
Torrid aggression,
That totally detests.

Being assertive is
Like being awake.
Corrupted fear of
Making a mistake.

Tall men in uniforms
Bursting their way through.
Fatal aggression
Is their only clue.

Fear has no
Respect of persons.
Boiling like an egg
Causing major diversions.

Internally weak,
Overcome by fear,
Fighting for survival,
Like a passive deer.

The sun never shines
On a fatal aggression.
Because of fear you
Would sign a confession.

Fatal aggression,
Centres in the mind.
Rush of adrenaline
Conquers mankind.

Do not be stupid,
Do not be glum.
Avoid aggression,
Avoiding a slum.

Another boring day,
Leads to a session.
Out of your mind,
Fatal aggression.

The bigger you are,
The more pain you afflict.
Fatal, progressive disease
Has you completely tricked.
Fear of incarceration,
Fear of being set free.
Fatal aggression is
Living in self-captivity

Hire a bodyguard.
You might live longer.
Fatal aggression is a negative
Energy making you feel stronger.

Fatal aggression is
Dangerous and distressing.
Fatal aggression,
Fatal aggression,
A counselling session,
Can help this fatal aggression.

Fatal aggression,
Fatal aggression.

Eternal Flame

A never-ending world
That is always turning.
A light in the dark as an
Eternal flame is burning.

All alone on a cold,
Wet winter's night.
Surviving the wilderness,
An eternity that's out of sight.

Like *déjà vu* we have
Been here a time before.
An everlasting life that,
Never closes its sacred door.

Reflecting on life, fear we
Will be forgotten not dead.
Leaving a life of sadness,
Like a corroding thread.

An eternity may not
Resume in a wonderland.
We will live forever in an
Eternity, we don't understand.

In our past life we
Thought was a game.
Renewing our souls
Of hurt and shame.

As the flame burns
It is healing with love,
On a starlit night,
From the powers above.

Walk through nature or
Listen to a running stream.
Away from life's chaos,
From a nightmare to a dream.

It's hard to believe a
Beginning with no end.
To an eternal life we
Hope to transcend.

As were passing we,
Should let go of shame.
We are being forgiving
Through an eternal flame.

As we close our eyes and,
See ourselves as the light.
A happier existence is
Almost in our sight.

In our humanity try
And let go of blame.
For we are being forgiving,
Through an eternal flame.

Let go, live free
With tranquillity.
We can tame
With an eternal flame.
Seek a higher power,
For every eternal hour.
On an eternal flame,
We are all the same.
I will always have a name,

With an eternal flame.
An eternal flame.
Eternal flame.
Eternal flame

A Bottomless Pit

As reality is futile and
Life is no longer legit,
On a roller-coaster ride
To find a bottomless pit.

In a world so sceptical,
It's hard to see an advance.
As we climb life's stairway,
With ambition and romance.

Drowning in a sea of alcohol,
The taste is so bittersweet.
Another bottle is a lifeboat,
Thinking our mission's complete.

Where's our family and friends,
Where has everyone gone?
We should have listened to
Their concerns at the break of dawn.

Like spinning in a whirlpool,
Showing no fear or emotion.
Cunning, baffling and powerful,
Alcohol is like a magic potion.

Feeding that adrenaline
As a form of an escape,
Thinking we are winning,
We're really out of shape.

No matter if we have fear
Of losing or winning,
Hitting a bottomless pit,
Could be a new beginning.

We can always dig our
Hole deeper and deeper,
Until we pass away and
Face the grim reaper.

We just need to keep on going,
As we will always make a mistake.
To survive a bottomless pit is a
Miracle not just a lucky break.

Caught up in hysteria and
Resentment's venomous bite.
In our bottomless pit we
Should reach to the light.

They might have seen us
Standing there all on our own,
A beggar feeding off scraps,
Like a hobo dog with a bone.

The best way to embrace our
Recovery and try get spiritually fit,
To come to the realisation of our
Reality that we are in a bottomless pit.

When we're bankrupt in
Every area of our life,
Throw in the towel. Think of
Our children, husband, or wife.

If we are players in a so-called
Game, we may not come back.
To survive a bottomless pit we
Must defend every wave of attack.

This is life we can't forfeit,
Another bottomless pit.
If we try to fly away,
We'll live to fight another day.
Be gentle put away the whip,
It's hard enough on this ghost ship.
Everyone is weary and wants to get well,
And get salvation from their prison cell.
Surrender to win,
For our journey to begin.
For ourselves do our bit,
In our bottomless pit.

A bottomless pit.
A bottomless pit.
Bottomless pit.

Urban Uprising

Societies derelict over
A distorted spell.
An urban uprising
Is beginning to tell.

Classed as underdogs,
In a life of crime,
A form of discrimination,
Urban area has done its time.

An uprising is to pull
Something from the mire.
To save an urban area,
Cool down, put out the fire.

Look up, look out,
Look from within,
Redeem oneself,
And conquer sin.

Guns and bombs explode,
As terrorism ceases.
Our human pride has
Been torn to pieces.

So many talents and gifts
That have gone wrong.
With this urban uprising
We feel we finally belong.

Hidden away amongst a
Tree of a wretched thorn.
If we play the victims,
We are liable for a scorn.

This urban rising is about
Camaraderie and being wise.
As a spiritual resurrection,
Together we believe and rise.

For every little thing we do,
To each little step we take,
This journey to a promise,
Land we will not forsake.

It's like were in automatic,
As we release our heavy load.
In this urban uprising we have,
Cracked and solved a magic code.

Wishing each other well,
Giving one and other a hug.
For all the pain and suffering,
We finally pulled out the plug.

This urban uprising is not,
As white as snow,
A lot of bridges to build,
And resentments to let go.

Listen inwards and outwards,
As the final whistles sounds.
We can live in harmonious peace,
That our sorrow slowly drowns.

Wake up, wake up, wake up,
Everything seems surprising.
Born again to new beginnings,
Blind faith of our urban uprising.

Keep going forward, never
Shut the door on the past.
Strive for equality and our
Uprising will forever last.

Rise up, rise.
To each day.
Rise up, rise,
On our way.

No need for
Advertising
Of egotism of
Urban uprising.

Look back and
See the cries.
Look forward
To see the rise.

It can be
Demoralising.
Mixed views of
An urban uprising.

Look up,
Look down.
Be positive,
Don't frown.

Be yourself,
No disguise.
Need a lift
Is to rise.

Urban rising, urban uprising,
Urban uprising.

Calming the Storm

As the different segments
Of society come out to play,
The stormy weather has come
To lead them in a state of disarray.

One hundred white horses
Gallop through the windy glen,
Trying to avoid the storm,
When it will end, or how it began.

Calm down, calm down
Are words used to calm a storm.
Whether you are alone in the cold,
Or living a life of luxury that's warm.

As the gates of safety are closing
On a storm that is losing time,
The fear of being caught in the
Storm as the clock ticks another chime.

Livelihoods of a community could
Be destroyed in less than an hour.
As hurricanes and cyclones have
Damaged our faith in a higher power.

Who believes in miracles or a
Magical World beyond a rainbow?
Is it an imagination of a dream?
Unless we look inside, we'll never know.

Reality is plagued with storms,
Of wars, corruptions and racism.
If we could all get on with our fellows,
There'd be less hatred and scepticism.

To survive a storm you may have to go
Through pain to reach the end line.
From a dark world of diseases,
To a world of healing and sunshine.

If you cannot afford your rent,
And you are facing an eviction,
You cannot calm the storm, because
Your money is spent on an addiction.

If your team is being battered,
And it's half time in the game,
To calm the storm is a good team talk,
Changing tactics and no one is to blame.

One hundred white horses galloping
Through a valley and a sunshine river.
We have survived the calming of the storm,
To bring our loved ones to safety that we'd deliver.
Calm the storm,
To be free and warm.
At the end of a rainbow,
We found peace and let go.
Calming of the storm.

Crocodile Tears

As a kid growing up,
Life was like a dream.
Then you see things,
That affected your esteem.

Bereavements and sickness,
Your spirit still could not awake.
You cried crocodile tears because
Of pain and fear of a heartbreak.

Wake up and smell the roses,
As the writing is on the wall.
Let go of your distorted perception,
If you don't want crocodile tears to fall.

Constant worry of worldly clamours,
Finance and romance are every season.
As your heart pleads insanity for
Crocodile tears are selfish without reason.

In a river is the rapacious crocodile,
Heartless and always on the prowl.
On a dark night you would want to
Be alert and as patient as an owl.

Like a panther in the wilderness
Hunting a pack of harmless deer.
Would you anticipate the worse
For them and shed some crocodile tears.

When your happy, joyous and free,
And you're in touch with feelings of love,
Forever heartache there is healing as
Crocodile tears are not cried from above.

You cannot escape a heartbeat for
If it stops beating, from life you refrain.
All those memories and loved ones,
Cry tears of joy, sadness and feel the pain.

Perhaps you're in a breakup in a marriage,
With your soul companion and sweetheart.
You still cry crocodile tears because you
Could not reach or melt your cold, cold heart.

Imagine the lover of your dreams who
Has on you a loving, romantic crush.
There is no room or time for crocodile tears,
As you feel the love and adrenaline rush.

Hope your heart cheers,
For no more crocodile tears.
Travelling in a Tunnel of Love,
Our hearts fit like a glove.
Tribal warriors hunts with spears,
To kill away the crocodile tears.
As you look so deep, deep,
Of love your heart will weep.
Keep your heart as an open door,
You may cry of love forever more.

Crocodile tears, crocodile tears,
Crocodile tears.

Seek The Rainbow's End

When I am alone and
In need of a friend,
I look to the sky and
Seek the rainbow's end.

So, intriguing I believe
In a colourful marriage.
An Empress awaits
In a golden carriage

A rainbow's end
Is what I seek.
Fairy-tale of wonder.
Magnificent, mystique.

Waking up along a
Colourful steam.
From a nightmare,
To a magical dream.

Diamonds sparkle
In a golden palace,
With no prejudice,
And no malice.

Beyond the heavens
And the blue sky,
In a land of truth
There are no lies.

Everyone is equal and
Has a golden star.
Just be yourself,
You will go far.

If any wickedness comes
To cast an evil spell,
The wizards can cast
It into a forgotten shell.

In a land of fantasy,
You must have faith.
That our loved ones are
beyond the pearly gates.

On a starlit night beyond
The realms of galactic space,
Normality has vanished
As the rainbow leaves no trace.

In the valley below
And the mountain high,
You must come back
Home as your loved ones cry.

As you seek to find the
Magic of the rainbow's end.
Just look inside your heart,
To divine love you will transcend.

Follow that glow,
Chase the rainbow.
Play hide and seek,
Strong or weak.
Live and let go,
Or else seek the rainbow.
In this magical show,
Of the rainbow's flow.
In your mind pretend,

You've reached a rainbow's end.
If the rainbow's end you find,
You may leave the world behind.

Seek the rainbow's end,
Seek the rainbow's end.
You have a newfound friend,
At the beginning of a rainbow's end.
A rainbow's end,
A rainbow's end
Rainbow's end.

Symphony of A Rag Town

Late to bed,
Early to rise.
Another rag day
Holds a surprise.

Like a Groundhog Day
With a different routine.
Any spare change
In this movie scene?

Boxing so clever
Like a needy fox
In a rag town
Of hard knocks.

Like a fallen leaf
Blowing in the wind.
Could I turn anew
Of a life so sinned?

As the rain pours,
Washing away my fears,
Helping me survive,
These strange atmospheres.

Getting moved on
To another bate,
In this symphony
That's too late.

In this rag town
Are puppets on a string.
Perceptions are distorted
Of a reality so embarrassing.

We have got to fight
To survive skid row.
A symphony that never ends,
Keeps on going with the flow.

Even the Godly
Turn away as
A poor unfortunate
Goes further astray.

Where is the justice,
Where is the hope?
Faith without light.
Is so hard to cope.

A symphony of people.
Who are down on their luck.
Can't reach for help.
In this rag town they are stuck.

In the darkness
Is a starlit night,
Like a blind person
Regains their sight.

A bitter symphony
That is so sweet.
As heroes and Villains
Try and survive the street.

Whatever reasons were,
We're still human beings.
Our gauntlet features
Takes us to unknown extremes.

To whom it concerns,
If you get a chance,
To look and listen at
This rag town stance.

So, close your eyes,
And follow suit.
Below the surface
May be the hidden truth.

Tis like we're all jesters
Fighting for a crown
In this symphony
Of a rag town.
Rag town, rag town,
My rag town,
I love this rag town.
Help ease my frown,
As they lay me down
To the symphony of a rag town.
Rag town, Rag town,
I love this rag town.
Our pride is our town,
Symphony of a rag town.
A rag town, A rag town,
A rag town.

The Bottle

I reach for the
Bottle every day.
It helps me function
And get on my way.

The bottle is my best
And abnormal friend,
Helps me to have peace,
To a better place I transcend.

All I can think of is
Where's my next drink?
On stormy seas of a
Shipwreck I will sink.

If only life was not
Complicated and tough
To function in society,
One bottle is never enough.

At the beginning it was
Harmless drinking in the park.
As it progressed it got worse,
Light was overshadowed by dark.

Like a magic trick everything,
In my life was gone vanished.
To survive skid row or try and
Control this disease and be banished.

How will I ever be able
To look the World in the eye.
Put one foot in front of the
Other keep giving it another try.

I am realising my powerlessness
Over this infatuation of a bottle.
I am heading for big trouble if
I don't take my foot off the throttle.

Where is all the glamour
And big city lights gone.
Faded away with a light
That may never come back on.

I love the bottle so much I'd
Rather go to jail or go insane.
Have the delirium tremens,
Or eventually get a wet brain.

Stop and think,
Before I take a drink.
Break out of this spell,
All alone in a prison cell.
Don't go to the end of the line
For a bottle of whiskey or wine.
It's like a new start or being reborn,
Away from all the trouble hurt I am scorn.
All my score cards read zero,
Put away the bottle, be my own hero.

Awakening of a Wake

As the people gather round the funeral home,

To see a loved in a casket with nowhere to roam.

Hearts drenched in sorrow and in floods of tears,

Reminiscing with care and joy reflected through the years.

In this ritual of a wake just like old pagan times,

The deceased gets judged by their actions and crimes.

We all sigh for forgiveness as the hurt and pain goes deeper,

Lurking in the shadows is the angel of death, the grim reaper.

It may take three days for the grim reaper to finally decide,

As the destination of the deceased is on-going and open wide.

For the lonely family's cry, its either a famine or a feast,

Will the spirit go above to the heaven or down below to the beast?

How the loved ones mourn is how the
grim reaper may judge,

Good memories and forgiveness, or bad repute
and holding a grudge.

A light of hope maybe of hand,
Or darkness may cover the land.
Repent this soul says the priest,
To the heavens it may be released.
Everyone is awakened at the wake,
For the grim reaper's decision to make.
Seek forgiveness to go to a better place,
The grim reaper is around we cannot trace.
Until death do part and to ever eternal life,
A lighted candle may heal your pain and strife.

I will set you free,
From captivity.
Because of this wake,
I shall not forsake.
For I am the grim reaper,
Sometimes love goes deeper,
Awakening of a wake,
Awakening of a wake.
Of a wake.

Haiku

Colours of a Rainbow

As darkness abides,
Colourful rainbow ignites.
Natures awaken.

Magical Sky

Rain shower passes.
Magical rainbow appears.
Imagination.

Beyond the Rainbow

A magical land
Begins at the rainbow's end.
Beyond the rainbow.

Painting a Picture

Colours so brightful
Of feelings delightful.
Painting a picture.

Captivating Image

Just one look it took,
Captivating perception.
Powerful image.

Interpretation

Whatever you see,
Positive or negative
Interpretation.

Colours of Miracles

Colours so faithful.
Healing from the other side.
Miracles of mind.

Saviour of Reality

Lifting our spirits.
Different opinions.
Colours that save us.

Infatuation

We can't comprehend.
We're always left to ponder.
Infatuation.

A Dream

Rainbow is a dream.
Scared of never waking up.
Dream and nightmare.

At the Earth's Core

There must be more life,
Magical, mysterious,
More at the Earth's core.

The Other Side

To go way beyond,
Like the oceans open wide,
Of the other side.

Another World

In another world,
No identification.
Euphoric recall.

Darkness to Colour

A new perception:
Magical enlightenment,
Like a promised land.

Love in Another Place

With faith I can face
To love in another place.
Gone without a trace.

A Golden Sprinkle of Stars

Shine in the night sky
Catching sprinkles in your eye,
Sailing on by.

A Fairy-Tale

Freedom of a whale
Resembles a fairy-tale.
Seek the holy grail.

Diamonds and Gold

We'd never grow old.
Everlasting life was sold.
Diamonds and gold.

A Crystal Maze

A hypnotic craze
To escape a crystal maze
Of eternal strays.

Futuristic Dimensional

Three dimensional
Colours of a rainbow.
There's no place like home.

Limericks

(I)

Maybe somewhere far beyond the clouds,

Is a magical kingdom with the jolliest crowds.

They live only with kindness, laughter and love,

In your dreams sail away to a fairy-tale from above.

You can never fail coz of each other,
everyone is proud.

(II)

There is nothing as captivating as a rainbow,

Colours of healing giving us a warmth and a glow.

It is somewhere we can never reach or transcend,

A mystery that no one has ever found
the rainbow's end.

Gaze in amazement and go the way the
wind may blow.

(III)

In life there is fiction or non-fiction,

Looking at the rainbow is like an addiction.

Once you see it you cannot get enough.

Anticipation of it can be smooth or rough,

Overflowing your imagination with friction.

(IV)

There was a Young Boy who was afraid of the dark,

One day he stumbled upon a rainbow in the park.

The multicolours changed his perception and sight.

He is no longer afraid and is tougher than dynamite.

Journey on a new life he can now try and embark.

(V)

There was a girl who found a magic wand,

She cast a spell that she would go far beyond.

In this fantasy world as she started to roam,

Suddenly realising there is no place like home.

She woke up to reality and a new day had dawned.

(VI)

When you feel down and life is passing you by,

A rainbow appears and lights up the dull sky.

You almost felt that there is no more hope,

Colours so illuminating gives you strength to cope.

Feel the despair and do not feel ashamed to cry.

(VII)

There once lived a king who lost his crown,

Instead of looking up he was looking down.

In the throes of sorrow feeling his despair,

A rainbow appeared making his kingdom aware.

The king got back his crown and only lost his frown.

(VIII)

Somewhere over the rainbow where unicorns fly,

Wizards and sorcerers with magic in their eyes,

Magic potions and druids that make you scream:

Is it a fiction of your imagination or is it a dream?

A rainbow is your guiding colours that light the sky.

(VIIII)

As the girl looked to the sky from her room,

She seen a witch fly on her magical broom.

Thinking to herself this is stranger than a dream,

Sailing to a strange land as she floats down a stream.

Beyond the moon and stars, she quicky went zoom.

(X)

There was a witch called Whinny the Wonderful.

She had a warm heart in a land so bitter and dull.

The other witches taunted her giving her a hard time,

All the spells she cast were of a good warm rhyme.

On a cold, frosty night, she could turn straw into wool.

Songs

Hello Darling

(Chorus)
Hello darling,
I hear you calling.
Hello darling,
I come crawling.
Hello darling,
Yeah, hello darling.
Hello darling.

Verse
(1)
Since we first met
Down through the years,
You opened my heart,
To cry a river of tears.

Verse
(2)
It's that warmth and glow,
Of your loving face.
You set me on fire,
With a stunning embrace.

(Chorus)
Hello darling,
I hear you calling.
Hello darling,
I come crawling.
Hello darling,
Yeah, hello darling.
Hello darling.

Verse

(3)

You changed my perception,
With just one look.
In a world ever changing
Like another chapter of a book.

Verse

(4)

I will give you the cream
Of my finest cake.
The moon and stars
I no longer forsake.

(Chorus)
Hello darling,
I hear you calling.
Set me free,
From hypocrisy.
Shine a light,
On this stage fright.
No more stalling,
Hello darling.

Verse
(5)
Meeting you darling,
Was a string to my bow.
Like a neon sign,
Showed me the way to go.

(Chorus)
Hello darling,
I hear you calling.
Hello darling,
I come crawling,
Hello darling,
Yeah, hello darling.
Hello darling

A Never-Ending Show

(Chorus)
A life that has no end,
You gotta go with the flow.
As the curtains come down
Of a never-ending show.
Listen to your sister,
Listen to your bro.
The show is never-ending.
We told you so.

Verse

(1)

Life is not a game,
We still gotta play.
A show so captivating,
Has taken us away.

Verse

(2)

We will stay until the end,
Until the final whistle blows.
Good and bad characters,
Of role models we chose.

(Chorus)

A life that has no end,
You gotta go with the flow.
As the curtains come down,
Of a never-ending show.
Listen to your sister,
Listen to your bro.
The show is never-ending,
We told you so.

Verse

(3)

Behind the backbeat,
Everyone is getting high.
It's a never-ending show.
To this we testify.

Verse

(4)

The show is like a jungle,
We're all trying to survive.
Back to the start,
We flock to the beehive.

Verse

(5)

We could make a million bucks
In this dirty old town.
The jester is the main act
As he stole the King's crown.

(Chorus)

A life that has no end,
you gotta go with the flow.
As the curtains come down,
Of a never-ending show.
Listen to your sister,
Listen to your bro.
The show is never-ending,
We told you so,
We told you so,
A never-ending show,
A never-ending show.
Yeah, we told you so,
Told you so.

A Starlit Night

(Chorus)
A cool chill of contentment,
In darkness there is light.
Christmas bells are ringing,
On a starlit night.
Listening in silence,
To our saviour's voice,
In the essence of time,
So accurate and precise.
A starlit night.
A starlit night.

Verse
(1)
Snowflakes are fallen,
Upon this wonderland.
A time of goodwill,
Giving a helping hand.

Verse

(2)

Rejoicing festivities,
Under the moonlight.
Calmness personified,
Of a starlit night.

(Chorus)
A cool chill of contentment,
In darkness there is light.
Christmas bells are ringing,
On a starlit night.
Listening in silence,
To our saviour's voice,
In the essence of time,
So accurate and precise,
On a starlit night.
A starlit night.

Verse

(3)

The Christmas spirit,
Is like water to the soul.
The magic of a starlit night,
Makes the world feel whole.

Verse

(4)

All the bad feelings and
Disappointments will disappear.
Letting go of the old, looking
forward to peaceful new year.

(Chorus)

A cool chill of contentment,
In darkness there is light.
Christmas bells are ringing,
On a starlit night.
Listening in silence.
To our saviour's voice.
In the essence of time,
So accurate and precise.
On a starlit might,
A starlit night.

Verse

(5)

Don't be afraid to be happy.
Let go of your sorrowful tears,
The wonder of a starlit night.
Will take away your blinded fears.

(Chorus)
A cool chill of contentment,
In darkness there is light.
Christmas bells are ringing,
On a starlit night.
Listening in silence,
To our saviour's voice,
In the essence of time,
So accurate and precise.
On a starlit night,
A starlit night.
The world is bright,
On a starlit night.
Shepherd's delight,
On a starlit night.
A starlit night.

A Rainbow's End

(Chorus)
At the end of the Earth's core,
Where can we transcend,
Colours so magical, and mystique
Of a rainbow's end.
Can we comprehend,
A rainbow's end,
A rainbows end?

Verse

(1)

A rainbow's end,
Could never be sold,
To light the darkness and
Bestow upon a pot of gold.

Verse

(2)

Beyond the dullness,
We're free of pain,
In a Land of fantasy,
Pours of magical rain.

(Chorus)
At the end of the Earth's core,
Where can we transcend,
Colours so magical, and mystique
Of a rainbow's end.
Can we comprehend
A rainbow's end?
A rainbow's end.

Verse

(3)

In a land of make believe,
Quicker than a blink of the eye,
It's like you've been here before,
And fallen from a dream in the sky.

Verse

(4)

Witches and ghouls
That go bump in the night,
Fairy godmothers with wands
Guiding a way of light.

(Chorus)

At the end of the Earth's core

Where can we transcend

Colours so magical, and mystique

Of a rainbow's end.

Can we comprehend,

A rainbow's end?

A Rainbows end.

Verse

(5)

Leprechauns dancing to

Music of a rainbow's pride.

Once you think it's a dream,

You will wake up to another side.

(Chorus)

At the end of the Earth's core,

Where can we transcend

Colours so magical. and mystique

Of a rainbow's end?

Can we comprehend

A rainbow's end?

A rainbow's end.

All it may take
Is a dream
To be part
Of life's team.

In your loneliness,
In need of a friend,
Look beyond the stars,
To a rainbow's end.

A rainbow's end,
A rainbow's end.

Dear Norah

(Chorus)
Dear Norah,
my Norah,
Norah,
You are my sunshine,
In the pouring rain.
Lifting, my spirit,
Through the pain.
Oh Norah,
My dear Norah.
Dear Norah

Verse
(1)
Like a river in flow,
You are water to my soul.
Calming the storm,
As it gets out of control.

Verse

(2)

Setting me free from,
From these lonely walls.
Away from my brokenness,
As the voice of an angel calls.

(Chorus)
Dear Norah,
My Norah,
Norah.
You are my sunshine,
In the pouring rain.
Lifting my spirit,
Through the pain.
Oh Norah,
My dear Norah.
Dear Norah.

Verse

(3)

So very intelligent,
Yet so ever humble.
Like a princess, you
Make the world crumble.

Verse

(4)

To all the people in your life,
You are a bright spark.
Guiding us on our way as
On a new journey we embark.

Verse

(5)

For those you have loved
That have passed away
Are smiling down with the Sun,
Guiding you to never go astray.

(Chorus)
Dear Norah,
My Norah,
Norah.
You are my sunshine,
in the pouring rain,
Lifting my spirit,
Through the pain.
Oh Norah,
My dear Norah,
My Norah

We adore
Dear Norah,
Could not ask,
For much more,
From our dear Norah.

Our ship has
Come to shore,
Thanks to faith,
And dear Norah.
Dear Norah

Old-School

(Chorus)
Old-school, old-school,
Old-school baby.
Times are changing,
There is a golden rule.
Never underestimate or
forget the old-school.
The old-school, old-school,
Yeah old-school.

Verse
(1)
Each decade is changing,
What use to be our school prom.
Is now a cocktail of alcohol and drugs,
Have we forgotten where we are from?

Verse
(2)
Technology is advancing,
Not everyone plays by the rules.
The best days of our lives came when
We were streetwise in the old-school.

(Chorus)
Old-school, old-school,
Old-school baby.
Times ae changing,
There is a golden rule.
Never underestimate or
Forget the old-school.
The old-school, old-school,
Yeah old-school.

Verse
(3)
You have got to be streetwise,
Without an exam or a test.
To survive a modern-day jungle,
Old-school is sharper than the rest.

Verse
(4)
Are modern-day footballers,
More skilful than those of the past?
With their stardom and lavish lifestyle,
Or the old-school which will forever last.

(Chorus)
Old-school, old-school,
Old-school baby,
Times are changing,
There is a golden rule.
Never underestimate or
Forget the old-school.
The old-school, old-school,
Yeah old-school.

Verse

(5)

Like a stream we roll along,
It can be chaos, or it can be cool,
Through the heartache we live and, play,
Our winning game which is old-school.

(Chorus)
Old-school, old-school,
Old-school baby,
Times are changing,
There is a golden rule.
Never underestimate or
Forget the old-school.

The old-school, old-school,
Yeah old-school.

Society can be cruel,
Even in the old-school.
Each of us is like a tool,
Living as one in the old-school.
Old-school, the old-school.

Voices in Our Heart

Verse

(1)

Music is soothing to the mind and soul,
It's the voices in our heart make us whole.
Our voices may be broken in time,
Music is healing of rhythm & rhyme.

Verse

(2)

Voices in our heart are cries of peace,
Coping with pain which will never cease.
Music reminds us of who we are,
Voices in our heart is like a guiding star.

Chorus

Voices are in our heart, as we can't speak,
making us strong when we're weak.
our hearts sing to a heavenly beat,
Inside we are dancing on the street.

Verse

(3)

The dark shadows make us feel doubt.

Our inner voices speak and shout.

Music is our wealth. Not money, or gold.

We will sing forever until too weak and old.

Verse

(4)

Feeling comfort as the music will play,

As our voices were fading away.

Beyond the rainbow way up above,

Our hearts have been inspired of a divine love.

Chorus

Voices are in our heart as we can't speak,

Making us strong when we're weak,

Our heart sings to a heavenly beat,

Inside we are dancing on the street.

Voices in our heart,

Plays a big part.

Listening to a tune,

Is like being on the moon.

We can feel at ease,
With Parkinson's disease.
Voices in our heart,
Voices in our heart,
In life we can take part
Because of voices in our heart.
In our heart.
Yeah.

The Road Home

(Chorus)
Lost in a reality which
Is no pleasure dome.
Injection on a highway
To find the road home.
Wearing a mask to
Find a new story,
A distorted society,
That has lost its glory.
Take the road home,
The road home.
Sweet home,
Wanna go home,
Home.

Verse
(1)
Take the road home
At your own pace.
Seek some guidance,
it's a journey not a race.

Verse

(2)

All the roads you
Must travel.
The more wreckage
You may have to unravel.

(Chorus)
Lost in a reality which
Is no pleasure dome.
Injection on a highway
To find the road home.
Wearing a mask to
Find a new story,
A distorted society,
That has lost its glory.
Take the road home,
The road home.
Sweet home,
Wanna go home.
Home.

Verse

(3)

In a ship you could
Sail the seven seas,
A journey that could
Turn at a hundred degrees.

Verse

(4)

Beyond a rainbow,
Maybe a way to return
From an unknown world,
Making your stomach churn.

Verse

(5)

One day it will
Be written in stone
That the journey of life
Should not be travelled alone.

(Chorus)

Lost in a reality which
Is no pleasure dome.

Injection on a highway
To find a road home.
Wearing a mask to
Find a new story,
A distorted society,
That has lost its glory.
Take the road home,
The road home.
Sweet home,
Wanna go home.
Home.

Growing Older

(Chorus)
Growing, growing older.
Memories of hardship
Upon our shoulder.
We can never stay
Forever young.
The birds of the past
Have already sung.
Move on, grow up,
As we grow older.
Growing older,
Growing older.

Verse

(1)

Playing a part in life
As a toy soldier.
Hard to understand
What is real, growing older.

Verse

(2)

Reflecting on life
As we're old and grey.
Missing our siblings
Who have passed away.

(Chorus)
Growing, growing older.
Memories of hardship
Upon our shoulder.
We can never stay
Forever young,
The birds of the past
Have already sung.
Move on, grow up,
As we grow older.
Growing older.
Growing older.

Verse

(3)

Some people believe
That they will live forever.

Sailing with ease through
The stormy weather.

Verse
(4)
The more we travel
We are harder to trace.
Growing older in life
Is a warm embrace.

Verse
(5)
As we look back, we
Repent and forgive.
Because we're growing,
We had a chance to live.

(Chorus)
Growing, growing older.
Memories of hardship
Upon our shoulder.
We can never stay
Forever young ...
The birds of the past,

Have already sung.
Move on, grow up,
As we grow older.
Growing older.
Growing older.

Every family tree
Has a destiny.
That life must end
For me and you, my friend ...
Travel to afar
On a shooting star.

Growing older,
Growing older,
Growing older.

Warmth of an Angel

(Chorus)
Angel, angel.
Warmth of an angel.
Sweet angel.
Oh angel.
In a battle,
Through a storm,
Presence of an angel,
So tender and warm.
Divine love so pure,
Feeling safe and secure.
Angel, angel.
My angel, angel.
Angel.

Verse

(1)

Down and out,
Full of despair.
Vision of an angel,
Takes me from there.

Verse

(2)

Every day in life

I make a mistake.

Forgiveness and gratitude,

I cannot forsake.

(Chorus)

Angel, angel,

Warmth of an angel.

Sweet angel.

Oh angel.

In a battle,

Through a storm,

Presence of an angel,

So tender and warm.

Divine love so pure.

Feeling safe and secure.

Angel, angel.

My angel, angel.

Angel.

Verse

(3)

In the blue skies
Are the white clouds.
Warmth of an angel
Amidst the madding crowds.

Verse

(4)

Warmth of an angel,
We will never die.
Our spirits are touched
By a heavenly lullaby.

Verse

(5)

The gospel of humanity
Shall forever prevail.
On an angel's wing to
Our destination we set sail.

(Chorus)
Angel, angel
Warmth of an angel.

Sweet angel.
Oh angel.
In a battle.
Through a storm.
Presence of an angel,
So tender and warm.
Divine love so pure,
Feeling safe and secure.
Angel, angel,
My angel, angel.
Angel

Our wounded scars
Are beyond the stars.
Our hearts sing
To a heavenly King.
We get things wrong,
We always belong.
Warmth of an angel,
Of an angel, an angel.
Angel.

Alone and Lonely

(Chorus)
Alone, alone,
And lonely.
Always lonely.
At the end of
A lonely day
Leads to a
Lonely night.
Life's pleasures,
Have vanished
out of sight.
Alone, alone,
All alone
And lonely.

Verse
(1)
Standing alone as
Life passes me by,
Hiding from the sun,
Behind a dark sky.

Verse

(2)

In a world of laughter,
I only feel sorrow.
To escape from myself,
I beg, steal, and borrow.

(Chorus)
Alone, alone,
And lonely.
Always lonely.
At the end of
A lonely day
Leads to a
Lonely night.
Life's pleasures
Have vanished,
Out of sight.
Alone, alone,
All alone,
And lonely.

Verse

(3)

How much more
Can I take?
Drown my sorrow
For every mistake.

Verse

(4)

Nowhere to run,
Nowhere to hide,
To escape realities,
Roller-coaster ride.

(Chorus)
Alone, alone,
And lonely.
Always lonely.
At the end of
A lonely day
Leads to a
Lonely night.
Life's pleasures
Have vanished,

Out of sight.
Alone, alone,
All alone,
And lonely.

Verse

(5)

The only way I can
Travel is in my head.
As the whistle blows,
The light is turning red.

(Chorus)
Alone, alone,
And lonely,
Always lonely.
At the end of,
A lonely day,
Leads to a,
Lonely night.
Life's pleasures
Have vanished,
Out of sight.
Alone, alone,

All alone.
And lonely.

To loneliness I am prone.
Having faith, I am not alone.
Trudge the road to be free,
Shipwrecked in a stormy sea.

So lonely, lonely.
Alone and lonely.
Lonely

Little Bird

(Chorus)
Little bird, little bird,
Oh, little bird I could
Not listen or say a word
In a life so obscured.
It is me and a little bird.
Little bird, little bird,
My little bird.

Verse

(1)

Times are tough and
I am on my knees,
Spirit is lifted as
You sing in the trees.

Verse

(2)

As I wonder
To and fro,
Little bird
I love you so.

Flying upon
Your wing
Makes my heart
Flutter and sing.

(Chorus)
Little bird, little bird,
Oh, little bird, I could
Not listen or say a word.
In a life so obscured
It is me and a little bird.
Little bird, little bird,
My little bird.

Verse
(3)
I love it when you
Bounce and bop.
All on your own
On a treetop.

Verse
(4)
I will never
Forget the day

That you
Must fly away.

My true friend
At a rainbows end.

Verse
(5)
Looking inside
Makes me aware
That you won't
Always be there.

(Chorus)
Little bird, little bird,
Oh, little bird I could not
Listen or say a word.
In a life so obscured.
It is me and a little bird.
Little bird, little bird.
My little bird.

I feel cured
With a little bird.

Makes me belong,
Singing nature's song.

Little bird, little bird,
Little bird.

Kings On a Throne

(Chorus)
Working ourselves
To the bone,
We are Kings
On a throne.
It's not a
Mystery
Why we go
Down in history.
We will never
Die alone.
We're Kings
On a throne.
Kings on a
Throne.

(Verse)
(1)
In our hearts
And in our minds never
Fighting for people,
As time unwinds.

(Verse)

(2)

Listening to the bird,

Of freedom as it sings.

Like an angel taking

Us away on its wings.

(Chorus)

Working ourselves

To the bone.

We are Kings

On a throne.

It's not a

Mystery,

Why we go

Down in history.

We will never

Die alone.

We're Kings

On a throne.

Kings on a

Throne.

Verse

(3)

We may be judged
By our past.
Loyalty to our throne
Is how we will last.

Verse

(4)

Some emperors
Who rules the Earth.
Always want more
Since their day of birth.

Verse

(5)

We want the
Fighting to cease.
We are true Kings
Striving for peace.

(Chorus)
Working ourselves
To the bone.

We are Kings
On a throne.
It's not a
Mystery
Why we go
Down in history.
We will never
Die alone.
We're Kings
On a throne.
Kings on a
Throne.

Kings on arrival,
Fighting for survival.
Bringing justice to our land
As we make a decisive stand.
We hope and pray,
Our Kings will never fade away.
To happiness we are prone,
Because of our Kings on a throne,
Kings on a throne.

Summertime

(Chorus)
Summertime,
Oh, so sublime,
Blue skies,
Girls and boys
Having fun,
In the sun.
Jet away
On a holiday.
Summertime,
Summertime,
No time for crying.
Summertime.

Verse
(1)
The fresh smell,
Of cut grass.
Flowers bloom,
A different class.

Verse

(2)

Dark clouds,

Pass by.

Buzzy bees,

Catch your eye.

(Chorus)

Summertime,

Oh, so sublime.

Blue skies,

Girls and boys.

Having fun,

In the sun.

Jet away,

On a holiday.

Summertime,

Summertime.

No time for crying,

Summertime.

Verse

(3)

On a beach,

Feeling lazy.

Lying in a field,
Like a daisy.

Verse

(4)

Cool drinks to
Quench the thirst.
As your lucky bet
Comes in first.

Verse

(5)

Take me away on
A cool starlit night.
Memories of a
Summertime delight.

(Chorus)
Summertime,
Oh, so sublime.
Blue skies,
Girls and boys
Having fun,
In the sun.

Jet away,
On a holiday.
Summertime,
Summertime,
No time for crying.
Summertime.

Relax and have a rest,
On your summertime quest.

Words will rhyme,
n summertime.
Summertime,
Summertime,
In your prime,
Summertime.

Lazy Days

(Chorus)
Shining like a
Silver spoon.
Lounging on a
Sunny afternoon.
Not bothered by
The latest craze.
Happy enough
On my lazy days.
Cannot get things
Ready or done.
Just want to
Bathe in the sun.
Lazy days, Lazy days.
Oh, my Lazy days.

Verse

(1)

Anticipating with
Fear and dread.
Because I cannot
Make it out of bed.

Verse

(2)

Eating munchies
Until I bust,
On my armchair,
I have been cursed.

(Chorus)
Shining like a
Silver spoon.
Lounging on a
Sunny afternoon.
Not bothered by
The latest craze.
Happy enough
On my lazy days.
Cannot get things
Ready or done.
Just want to
Bathe in the sun.
Lazy days, lazy days,
Oh, my lazy days.

Verse

(3)

I cannot succeed,
Engage or initiate.
Keeping me in touch
With reality is my faith.

(Bridge)

Mending my ways
Of these lazy days.
Try stay in touch
As things get too much.
Get off this constant dream,
Build up some self-esteem.
Be happy and go free
from the despair of being lazy.

Verse

(4)

What about being
Healthy? What's the point?
Drink a few beers,
Smoke another joint.

Verse

(5)

We all have some
Sort of responsibility.
We will never fulfil our
paternal with incapability.

(Chorus)
Shining like a
Silver spoon.
Lounging on a
Sunny afternoon.
Not bothered by
The latest craze.
Happy enough
On my lazy days.
Cannot get things
Ready or done.
Just want to
Bathe in the sun.
Lazy days, lazy days,
Oh, my lazy days.
Change my ways,
Of lazy days.
Lazy days.

Rasta Rasta Rainbow

(Chorus)
In the darkness,
There is a glow.
Follow your dreams
And freedom with a
Rasta, rasta rainbow.
Colours so bright,
They always deliver.
Like a bridge in
The sky across
A magical river.
Rasta, rasta rainbow,
Rainbow, rainbow rasta.

Verse
(1)
It's sunshine
Through the rain.
No need to wait,
Or die in vain.

Verse

(2)

One look at it takes
Away your breath.
Like a miracle saving
You from your death.

(Chorus)
In the darkness,
There is a glow.
Follow your dreams
And freedom with a
Rasta, rasta, rainbow.
Colours so bright,
They always deliver
Like a bridge
In the sky across
A magical river.
Rasta, rasta, rainbow.
Rainbow, rainbow, Rasta.

Verse

(3)

Sail away to a
Rainbow's end.

Like a dream the Rasta
Man will be tranced.

Verse
(4)

For a Rasta man
Needs to get high
By gazing at a
Rainbow in the sky.

(Bridge)

Like Roses and wine,
A Rainbow is so divine.
We may make peace,
As a rainbow will never cease.
Look for a Rainbow and fly away,
For a Rasta man to see a better day.

Verse
(5)

Like a bluebird sing
Upon a treetop.
The curiosity of a
Rainbow will never stop.

(Chorus)
In the darkness,
There is a glow.
Follow your dreams,
And freedom with a
Rasta, rasta, rainbow.
Colours so bright,
They always deliver.
Like a bridge
In the sky across
A magical river.
Rasta, rasta, rainbow.
Rainbow, rainbow, rasta.
Rasta man is a friend,
At the rainbow's end.
Rasta, rasta, rainbow,
Rainbow, rainbow, rasta.

Troubled Times

(Chorus)
Troubled times,
Troubled times,
Oh, troubled times.
Like a ship sail
Upon stormy waters.
Rescuing from wreckage
Is our sons and daughters.
Troubled times,
Oh, troubled times,
Sign of the times.

Verse
(1)
Lessons in love,
We need to learn.
For broken hearts,
Worry with concern.

Verse

(2)

Moonlight reflects,
Upon the ocean.
In troubled times,
We show devotion.

(Chorus)
Troubled times,
Troubled times,
Oh, troubled times.
Like a ship sail,
Upon stormy waters.
Rescuing from wreckage
Is our sons and daughters.
Troubled times,
Oh, troubled times,
Sign of the times.

Verse

(3)

In departure or
You're in arrival.
Faith and a decision,
Could be your survival.

Verse

(4)

Down and out,
With no look.
In a whirlpool you
Cannot pass the buck.

(Bridge)

Love and hate crimes
Are of troubled times.
Very few people escape,
The barrel as they scrape.

Verse

(5)

Building a bridge
Over life's trouble.
Awoken to reality
Inside of a bubble.

(Chorus)

Troubled times,
Troubled times.
Oh, troubled times.

Like a ship sail,
Upon stormy waters.
Recuing from wreckage
Is our sons and daughters.
Troubled times,
Oh, troubled times.
Sign of the times.

Buried deep under the rubble,
Are generations scorned with trouble.

With all our airs and graces,
Better stay out of troubled places.

Sometimes we decline
And go to the endline.

Troubled times,
Oh, troubled times.

Mama Don't Go

(Chorus)
Don't go Mama.
Mama don't go.
We need you here
And we love you so.
Not forgetting the
Memories of the past.
Look to the light and away
From the darkness you are cast.
Don't go Mama.
Mama don't go.
Don't go Mama.

Verse

(1)

Mama, we love you so,
And you're always there.
You lightened up our hearts and
Of ourselves we became aware.

Verse

(2)

Looking on the bright side of
Life it seemed like a show.
With knowledge of life we
Need you here mama, don't go.

(Chorus)

Don't go mama.
Mama don't go.
We need you here
And we love you so.
Not forgetting the
Memories of the past.
Look to the light and away
from the darkness you are cast.
Don't go Mama.
Mam don't go.
Don't go Mama.

Verse

(3)

Looking deep
Inside of our roots.

With pride we swallow
Some home truths.

Verse

(4)

Even though you
Are old and frail,
You helped us to
Stay on the right trail.

(Bridge)

Like a river in flow,
Mama don't go.
Beyond a rainbow,
Mama don't go.
Mama don't go.

Verse

(5)

You'll always be our,
Queen of the Earth.
To fulfil our goals
You helped us assert.

(Chorus)
Don't go Mama.
Mama don't go.
We need you here,
And we love you so.
Not forgetting the
Memories of the past.
Look to the light and away
From the darkness you are cast.
Don't go Mama.
Mama don't go.
Don't go Mama.

Queen of our heart,
You played your part.
You will go to a sacred place.
In your footsteps, we'll trace …

Like a blooming flower,
You're a way to higher power.

Don't go Mama,
Mama don't go.
Don't go Mama.

Rise of the Underdog

(Chorus)
Through the dark
And misty fog
Is the rise of
The underdog.
As they kick us
While were down,
We get back up,
reclaiming our crown.
Underdog, underdog.
Yeah, rise of
The underdog.

Verse
(1)
In a chain gang it's
Hard to break the chain.
In a discriminated society,
We strive upon our pain.

Verse

(2)

A life lived in the slums,
It is hard to engage.
They didn't write us down,
But wrote us off the page.

(Chorus)
Through the dark
And misty fog
Is the rise of
The underdog.
As they kick us
While we're down,
We get back up
Reclaiming our crown.
Underdog, underdog,
Yeah, rise of,
The underdog.

Verse

(3)

Walking around with
Troubles on our shoulder.

They told us again and again
We'll fail when we're older.

(Bridge)
It's hard to understand,
Reaching out a helping hand.
Another hard day's slog,
Is a rise of the underdog.
With a lack of respect,
We will always resurrect.

Verse

(4)

To carry the burden
Of our family tree.
Rise of the underdog
Will always break free.

Verse

(5)

A million to one shot is
Almost impossible to win.
An underdog to rise, this
Is where it may have to begin.

(Chorus)
Through the dark
And misty fog
Is the rise of
The underdog.
As they kick us
While we're down,
We'll get back up,
Reclaiming our crown.
Underdog, underdog.
Yeah, rise of,
The underdog.
Underdog.
Underdog

The Cuckoo's Nest

(Chorus)
Cuckoo, cuckoo.
Cuckoo's nest.
Your mind is baffled
And you cannot rest.
As you check into
The cuckoo's nest.
It's spooked and
Full of superstition.
Out of the other side,
Of insanity is your mission.
Cuckoo, cuckoo,
Cuckoo's nest.

Verse
(1)
The cuckoo's nest
Is enthralling.
On your knees
You'll be crawling.

Verse

(2)

From reality you

Have lost touch.

Will you come back?

You're asking too much.

Verse

(3)

Mad men laughing

At the pouring rain,

Helps them escape

Humiliation and pain.

(Chorus)

Cuckoo, cuckoo,

Cuckoo's nest.

Your mind is baffled

And you cannot rest.

As you check into

The cuckoo's nest,

It's spooked and

Full of superstition.

Out of the other side

Of insanity is our mission.
Cuckoo, cuckoo.
Cuckoo's nest.

Verse
(4)
As the clock ticks
Upon the wall.
Wondering if any
Visitors will call.

Verse
(5)
The sound of voices
Inside of your brain,
Faster and louder
Than a runaway train.

(Bridge)
In this institution
Is a revolution.
So tired and lazy,
Everyone is acting crazy.
What have you done,
To grace the house of fun?

(Chorus)
Cuckoo, cuckoo,
Cuckoo's nest.
Your mind is baffled
And you cannot rest.
As you check into
The cuckoo's nest.
It's spooked and
Full of superstition.
Out of the other side
Of insanity is our mission.
Cuckoo, cuckoo,
Cuckoo's nest.
One day I will lay to rest
In the cuckoo's nest,
Cuckoo's nest.

Hometown

(Chorus)
In this hometown
We learn to wear
Life like a loose gown.
In a sea of memories
We slowly drown.
As we set sail to
Waken our hometown.
Hometown, hometown.
Yeah, our hometown.
Hometown.

Verse
(1)
At the crossroads
Of our destination.
Our chosen path is
Prior to investigation.

Verse

(2)

Breaking down the
Barriers that hold us inside.
To rebuild our hometown
Of its ancestor's pride.

(Chorus)
In this hometown
We learn to wear
Life like a loose gown.
In a sea of memories
We slowly drown.
As we set sail to
Awaken our hometown,
Hometown, hometown.
Yeah, our hometown.
Hometown.

Verse

(3)

Little by little,
We'll reach the top.
Our hometown is
Cream of the crop.

Verse

(4)

As the music
Begins to sway.
In this hometown
We'll find a way.

(Bridge)

A better place,
No more disgrace.
We have lucky calls
To scale the walls.

Verse

(5)

Class a drug in
All its trouble.
Break the chains,
Burst its bubble.

(Chorus)

In this hometown
We learn to wear
Life like a loose gown.

In a sea of memories
We slowly drown.
As we set sail to
Awaken our hometown.
Hometown, hometown.
Yeah, our hometown,
Hometown.

Ease our frown
In this hometown,
If it makes us laugh
Like an old photograph
We could never pawn,
As it leads to a new dawn.

Hometown,
Hometown.

Masters

(Chorus)
Masters, masters,
On the street.
Dealing with lies,
Truth and deceit.
Masters, masters,
You will find.
Unique and eccentric
Of a different kind.
Masters, masters,
Oh masters.

Verse
(1)
Plain sailing through
A stormy sea.
So diligent,
Wild and free.

Verse
(2)
Masters may
Not wear a crown.

But they look up,
And never look down.

Verse
(3)
A master will
Very rarely judge.
Calmest personified,
Never hold a grudge.

(Chorus)
Masters, masters,
On the street,
Dealing with lies,
Truth and deceit.
You will find
Unique and eccentric,
Of a different kind.
Masters, masters,
Oh masters.

Verse
(4)
Masters will climb
Branch after branch.

City slickers that
Live in a ranch.

(Bridge)
Masters are so slick
With a classy chic.
They still have style
At the bottom of the pile.

Verse
(5)
A master can be
Reeled in for bait,
Enduring hostility
With or without faith.

(Chorus)
Masters, masters,
On the street,
Dealing with lies,
Truth and deceit.
You will find
Unique and eccentric,
Of a different kind.

Masters, masters,
Oh masters.

Getting through disasters,
Warriors and masters.
Masters, masters,
Yeah masters.

Players

(Chorus)
Players, players,
They come and go,
The salt of the Earth,
Warmth in the snow.
Richness in faith not
By prestige or wealth.
Playing the perfect hand
That they are dealt.
Players, players,
Yeah players,
Players.

Verse
(1)
Toughness and wisdom
That can't be sold.
Kindness and love
In a heart of gold.

Verse

(2)

Players are allowed
To make a mistake.
Putting in a hard graft,
There is no lucky break.

Verse

(3)

Players are most
Charming lovers.
Coming back from a place
Where no one else recovers.

(Chorus)

Players, players,
They come and go.
The salt of the Earth,
Warmth in the snow.
Richness in faith not
By prestige or wealth.
Playing the perfect hand
That they are delt.
Players, players,
The players.
Players.

Verse

(4)

With a sharpness of,
Diamonds in their eyes.
They can see in the dark,
The true from the lies.

(Bridge)

Never ashamed to cry,
To say hello or wave goodbye.
In life they can enhance,
Don't believe in just one chance.
In accepting who they are,
Has carried society to afar.

Verse

(5)

Positive outlook is
They believe they can.
Not a one hit wonder
Or a flash in the pan.

(Chorus)

Players, players,
They come and go.

Salt of the Earth,
Warmth in the snow.
Richness is in faith not
By prestige or wealth.
Playing the perfect hand
That they are delt.
Players, players,
Yeah players.
Players.
They know no shame,
Humble in the halls of fame.
Something we cannot understand,
There's always a way to beat the band.
Players, players,
Oh players.

Crossing Over

(Chorus)
Crossing over, over,
To the other side.
Reflecting on a life
Of love and pride.
Crossing over beyond
A light of a crystal moon.
I am gone for now but
I will see you all soon.
Crossing over, over,
Like a wild rover.
Crossing over.

Verse
(1)
My destination is
Still so unknown.
Until this wake of gestures
And memories I am shown.

Verse

(2)

For those I loved there,
Hearts are no longer colder.
The spiritual realm has left
Hurt and pain off their shoulder.

Verse

(3)

I was a human being
With clay feet.
I am far above
Or far beneath.

(Chorus)
Crossing over, over,
To the other side.
Reflecting on a life
Of love and pride.
Crossing over beyond
A light of a crystal moon.
I am gone for now but
I will see you all soon.
Crossing over, over,
Like a wild rover.
Crossing over.

Verse

(4)

To meet my maker,
How long must it take
For the angel of death
To pardon and forsake...

(Bridge)

I need water to my soul,
Keep me from a dark hole.
My spirit will vanish without a trace,
To the afterlife I must embrace.

Verse

(5)

Tears you cry
Bring me relief,
To a place
Beyond belief.

(Chorus)

Crossing over, over,
To the other side.
Reflecting on a life

Of love and pride.
Crossing over beyond
A light of a crystal moon.
I am gone for now but
I will see you all soon.
Crossing over, over,
Like a wild rover,
Crossing over.

I hope to transcend
To a beginning not to an end.
Set my spirit free
From damnation of an eternity.

Crossing over, over,
Crossing over,
Crossing over.

Wild Horses

(Chorus)
Free as wild horses,
As wild horses,
Wild horses.
Like the comfort
Of human endorses.
It's the equivalent
Of freedom of
Running wild horses.
Stallions that gallop
Through the night.
The beauty of nature
Is never out of sight.
Run free as wild horses.
Wild horses,
wild horses.

Verse

(1)

Over mountains,
Through fields of green.
Wild horses are the best
Sight nature's ever seen.

Verse

(2)

Valliant animals

That show no fear.

Ghosts of the glen,

No obstacles they can't clear.

Verse

(3)

Cries of the wilderness

As nature bears its soul.

To the folk law and birth

Of another miracle's foil.

(Chorus)

Free as wild horses,

As wild horses,

Wild horses.

Like the comfort

Of human endorses.

It's the equivalent

Of freedom of

Running wild horses.

Stallions that gallop

Through the night,
The beauty of nature
Is never out of sight.
Run free as wild horses,
Wild horses,
Wild horses.

Verse

(4)

Dark shadows that
Keep nature alive.
From man's egotism
And wealth they strive.

Verse

(5)

Beyond this World is a
place where wild horses go.
A spiritual realm where
Horses spirits only know.

(Bridge)

In our dreams,
Running through streams,

Thoroughbreds so cool,
Are nature's golden rule.
Out there but not astray,
Wild horses will never fade away.

(Chorus)
Free as wild horses,
As wild horses,
Wild horses.
Like the comfort
Of human endorses.
It's the equivalent
Of freedom of
Running wild horses.
Stallions that gallop
Through the night.
The beauty of nature
Is never out of sight.
Run free as wild horses.
Wild horses.
Wild horses.
Ride with the wind
Though the storm.
Ride like the wind
Until it's safe and warm.

Wild horses run free
For the sake of humanity.
Ride on.
Ride free.
Wild horse.

A Gift

(Chorus)
A gift, a gift,
When others
Are down, you
Have a gift
Of a colourful smile
That gives a lift.
The way you
Listen and console
Is like fresh water
Cleansing the soul.
A gift, a gift.
A gift.

Verse
(1)
Never quit,
Never fail.
Gift of freedom
From life's jail.

Verse

(2)

Leaves on the trees
Will always grow.
Gift of sunshine as it
Melts the winter's snows.

Verse

(3)

Gift of a new-born
Baby's first cries.
A gift of honesty,
Where there are lies.

(Chorus)
A gift, a gift.
When others
Are down, you
Have a gift
Of a colourful smile
That gives a lift.
The way you
Listen and console
Is like fresh water

Cleansing the soul.
A gift, a gift,
A gift.

Verse

(4)

Full of talent
And of skill.
Gift of giving
Others a thrill.

(Bridge)

Gift of the latest craze
Or helping others out of a maze.
Gift of feeling someone else's pain,
A heart of gold and an intellectual brain.

Verse

(5)

Gift of being
Able to tell.
The difference between
Heaven and hell.

(Chorus)
A gift, a gift.
When others
Are down, you
Have a gift
Of a colourful smile,
That gives a lift.
The way you
Listen and console
Is like fresh water
Cleansing the soul.
A gift, a gift.
A gift.

Stopping others from
Going further adrift.
You have a special,
Special kind of gift.

A gift, a gift,
A loving gift.
A gift

Soulmate

(Chorus)
I am missing you,
Yeah, missing you,
My soulmate.
Like a light of
An eternal flame,
Those lights of faith
With love in my heart
And hope in my soul.
Now you're missing,
I have lost control.
I am missing you,
Yeah, missing you.
It's never too late,
My soulmate,
Soulmate.

Verse
(1)
My first love have
You forgotten
To unbreak my heart
Of a false love so rotten.

Verse

(2)

Has anyone seen you,
Earth angel of mine?
To survive all alone
Is almost death defying.

Verse

(3)

All I can do is
Flow with my tears.
Reflecting memories of
Life through the years.

(Chorus)

I am missing you.
Yeah, missing you.
My soulmate.
Like a light of
An eternal flame,
Those lights of faith
With love in my heart,
And hope in my soul.
Now you're missing,

I have lost control.
I am missing you,
Yeah, missing you.
It's never too late,
My soulmate.
Soulmate.

Verse

(4)

I guess all we had was
The sun, moon and stars.
True love never dies was
Healing both of our scars.

(Bridge)

From love I cannot refrain.
Missing you I feel the pain.
The very first day I had a crush.
With you I get an adrenaline rush.
Missing you my sweet sensation,
Why you left is prior to investigation.

Verse

(5)

On those cold nights
As I walked you home,
Now I am all alone
With no place to roam.

(Chorus)

I am missing you,
Yeah, missing you.
My soulmate.
Like a light of
An eternal flame,
Those lights of faith
With love in my heart,
And hope in my soul.
Now you're missing,
I have lost control.
I am missing you,
Yeah, missing you.
It's never too late
My soulmate,
Soulmate.

You're a Ghost

(Chorus)
You're a ghost, a ghost,
I see you're a ghost.
To true love,
We gave a toast.
Without you I thought
I would never survive.
Although you're gone,
Your spirit is alive.
My heart's filled
With sorrowful tears.
A euphoric recall reflecting
Through the years.
You're a ghost, a ghost.
I see you're a ghost.

Verse

(1)

Memories of you
Makes me shiver.
Messages from the
Afterlife you deliver.

Verse

(2)

I feel your presence
In the wind blowing.
You're watching over
Me, I sense you glowing.

Verse

(3)

A crystal heavenly
Light that you shine,
In a difficult time has
Helped me over the line.

(Chorus)

You're a ghost, a ghost,
I see you're a ghost.
To true love,
We gave a toast.
Without you I thought
I would never survive.
Although you're gone,
Your spirit is alive.
My heart's filled

With sorrowful tears,
A euphoric recall reflecting,
Through the years.
You're a ghost, a ghost,
I see you're a ghost.

Verse

(4)

Where we lived,
Along the coast,
Sound of the ocean,
I feel you're a ghost.

(Bridge)

Am I supposed
To love a ghost?
Oh, angel of mine,
Everything is fine.
To myself I will boast,
I see you're a ghost.
A ghost, a ghost,
You're a ghost.

Verse

(5)

I see your footprints
As we walk in the sand.
Together in the moonlight,
Walking hand in hand.

(Chorus)
You're a ghost, a ghost,
I see you're a ghost.
To true love
We gave a toast.
Without you I thought
I could never survive.
Although you're gone,
Your spirit is alive.
My heart's filled,
With sorrowful tears,
A euphoric recall,
Reflecting through the years.
You're a ghost, a ghost,
I see you're a ghost.

True love never dies,
Or hears ghostly cries.
Thanks for being there,
For making my spirit aware.
Healing pain of loves torn,
To a spiritual realm were reborn.

You're a ghost, a ghost,
I see you're a ghost.
A ghost, a ghost.
A ghost.

Oh Shari

(Chorus)
Shari, oh Shari,
Flowing like the breeze,
Free as the birds and bees.
Take me to a sacred place
So of this life I can embrace.
Shari, Oh Shari.

Verse
(1)
Between darkness and light
As life felt out of sight.
Dance the night away
Until the break of day.

Verse
(2)
I was blind, now I see,
Because you set me free.
Turning me upside down,
A Queen that needs no crown.

(Chorus)
Shari, oh Shari,
Flowing like the breeze,
Free as the birds and bees.
Take me to a sacred place
So of this life I can embrace
Shari, oh Shari.

Verse

(3)

You're a hidden treasure,
A golden sun of pleasure.
It's a journey to endeavour,
On a path to freedom forever.

Verse

(4)

Oh, Shari my sensation,
Heart and soul of the nation
I see you in my dreams,
Shining your heavenly beams.

(Chorus)
Shari, oh Shari,
Flowing like the breeze,

Free as the birds and bees.
Take me to a sacred place,
So, of this life I can embrace,
Shari, oh Shari.

Verse

(5)

An angel without wings,
For you my heart sings,
As a ship sails into the docks,
Healing my love on the rocks.

(Chorus)

Shari, oh Shari
Flowing like the breeze,
Free as the birds and bees.
Take me to a sacred place,
So, of this life I can embrace.
Shari, oh Shari,
Sweet Shari,
Oh Shari, Shari

Christmas Of Joy and Peace

(Chorus)
Christmas, Christmas,
Once again, it's Christmas.
A time to celebrate,
Of joy and peace.
As we open our hearts
That the fighting will cease.
The spirit of Christmas is
Upon us there's no stalling.
As children are excited that
Father Christmas is calling.
Christmas of joy,
Christmas of peace,
Merry Christmas.

Verse
(1)
Like a power
From above.
Touching us in
The form of a dove.

Verse

(2)

The peace of
a candlelight.
And magic of
A land so white.

Verse

(3)

A time for giving
At an honest cost.
To feel the coolness
And glow of Jack Frost.

(Chorus)
Christmas, Christmas,
Once again, it's Christmas.
A time to celebrate,
Of Joy and peace.
As we open our hearts
That the fighting will cease.
The spirit of Christmas is
Upon us. There's no stalling.
As children are excited that

Father Christmas is calling.
Christmas of joy.
Christmas of peace.
Merry Christmas.

Verse

(4)

Festive gathering
Of wine and song.
A time of love where
Everyone must belong.

(Bridge)

The world has been adored
Because of the birth of our Lord.
No time to be a slacker,
Come on pull us a cracker.
Under the mistletoe there is a kiss,
Happy Christmas of sheer love and bliss.

Verse

(5)

Looking down upon
A winter wonderland.

For our future we must
Be brave and make a stand.

(Chorus)
Christmas, Christmas.
Once again, it's Christmas.
A time to celebrate,
Of Joy and peace.
As we open our hearts
That the fighting will cease.
The spirit of Christmas is
Upon us there's no stalling.
As children are excited that
Father Christmas is calling.
Christmas of joy.
Christmas of peace.
Merry Christmas
And a happy new year.
We wish we can lease.
Merry Christmas.

A Jolly Christmas Time

(Chorus)
Have a jolly
Christmas time.
Whether you're
Old and grey,
Or young and
In your prime,
Rejoice everyone
And be jolly.
With mistletoe, wine,
And bowls of holly,
Have a jolly
Christmas time.
A jolly Christmas,
Christmas time.

Verse
(1)
Celebrate our
Saviours' day.
With the anticipation
Of Santa upon his sleigh.

Verse

(2)

Families playing
In the snow.
The whole world
Is white and aglow.

Verse

(3)

Open your
Heart and mind.
At Christmas no one
Should be left behind.

(Chorus)

Have a jolly
Christmas time.
Whether you're
Old and grey,
Or young and
In your prime,
Rejoice everyone
And be jolly.
With mistletoe, wine,

And bowls of holly,
Have a jolly
Christmas time.
A jolly Christmas,
Christmas time.

Verse

(4)

A time to wear
A feather in your cap.
At Christmas time there
Should be no poverty trap.

(Bridge)

We gaze and wonder of a starlit night,
A time for peace where no one should fight.
With passion in our hearts as the snow falls,
We flow with the river to the sound of the waterfalls.
Christmas time is jolly we should never forsake,
For our skin is aglow and our spirits are awake.

Verse

(5)

There are people who
Starve beneath the sun.

We think of them as we
Rejoice and have our fun.

(Chorus)
Have a jolly
Christmas time.
Whether poor,
Old and grey,
Or young and
In your prime,
Rejoice everyone
And be jolly.
With mistletoe, wine,
And bowls of holly.
Have a jolly
Christmas time.
A jolly Christmas,
Christmas time.

Happy Christmas,
Hope it's sublime.
Happy Christmas,
Have a jolly time.
Merry Christmas,
Christmas time.
Merry Christmas.

A Little Red Robin

(Chorus)
A little red robin
On a snowflake tree
Chirps, chirps, chirps,
Of glee, glee, glee.
A little red robin
On a snowflake tree
Chirps, chirps, chirps,
Of glee, glee, glee.
One look at that robin,
My heart goes a-throbbing.
Little Red Robin.
Red Robin.

Verse

(1)

Little red robin is
Like a wandering star.
Taking me beyond the
Moon to a place of afar.

Verse

(2)

Like a magical Christmas
Painted in a postcard,
Easing my troubles of a
Life which I cannot discard.

Verse

(3)

Little red robin when
You bounce and hop,
Takes me from the
Bottom to the top.

(Chorus)

A little red robin
On a snowflake tree
Chirps, chirps, chirps,
Of glee, glee, glee.
A little red robin
On a snowflake tree.
Chirps, chirps, chirps,
Of glee, glee, glee.
One look at that robin,

My heart goes a-throbbing.
Little red Robin.
Red Robin.

Verse

(4)

Like a diamond
Shining in the snow,
Awakens my spirit,
Helps me to let go.

(Bridge)

I look to a robin,
As my heart is sobbing.
Making me feel stronger,
At Christmas I am alone no longer.
Captivating Christmas time,
Little red robin you are sublime.

Verse

(5)

With your little twirps,
You are so sweet.
Brightening up the
Dark side of the street.

(Chorus)
A little red robin
On a snowflake tree
Chirps, chirps, chirps,
Of glee, glee, glee.
A little red robin,
On a snowflake tree
Chirps, chirps, chirps,
Of glee, glee, glee.
One look at that robin,
My heart goes a-throbbing.
Little red robin.
Red robin.
You mean so much to me
Upon a Christmas snowflake tree.
Little robin, little robin.
A little red robin.

Bibtidy, boptidy, biptidy, bop,
Hoptidy, hoptidy, hiptidy, hop.

A little red robin don't you ever stop
Capturing our imagination on a treetop.

A little red robin.
Little red robin,
Red robin.

Rap Poetry
Aristocrats

(Chorus)
Aristocrats, aristocrats,
Known as little rich brats.
In their corporate land,
They have the upper hand.
Aristocrats, aristocrats,
Aristocrats.

Verse

(1)

They say some have all the luck,
Lavish lifestyles that are starstruck.
Very few people start at the top,
No fear of making societies drop.
Want or need nothing except wealth,
Does never affect their mental health.
Aristocrats are warm and funny,
A little bit selfish concerning money.
They make a living through hard graft
Then make the ordinary look like they're daft.

Through time they had like royal marriages,
Glitz and glam with golden carriages.
They have a very persuading tone of voice,
To not do business we have lost our choice.
To know an aristocrat leaves an open door.
In the game of life, we can't predict the score.

(Chorus)
Aristocrats, aristocrats,
Known as little rich brats.
In their corporate land,
They have the upper hand.
Aristocrats, aristocrats,
Aristocrats.

Verse

(2)

Global success is baked in a big pie,
Some of it is sadness, some of it is joy.
An aristocrat is hard to try and outthink,
They are so clever. Their ship will never sink.
In a world of business sorrow slowly drowns,
Are we classed as hard workers or as clowns.
Follow the leaders wherever they may go,

As each segment of society has its own flow.
An aristocrat is as wise as an owl.
Give them the benefit, fair play or foul.
In the past as they gathered for a feast,
A celebration, or someone who has deceased,
As the employees seek justice waving a banner,
slavery means nothing to the Lord of the Manor.
If you see a man in s suit and a fancy top hat,
You could be swept away by an aristocrat.

(Chorus)
Aristocrats, aristocrats,
Known as little rich brats.
In their corporate land,
They have the upper hand.
Aristocrats, aristocrats,
Aristocrats.

Verse
(3)
Society may be of different classes,
As equality plays in the pipes and brasses.
If someone is wealthy they can be reassured
If they get sick or die, they will always be insured.

To see a light even if we are as blind as a bat,
Compliments and dedication of an aristocrat.
Will poverty and discrimination ever end?
To a promised land we hope to transcend.
A lot of workers work hard for little pay.
Has human kindness gone further astray?
Some live in luxury complaining about the nation,
Others are poor with no form of communication.
Politicians predict our lives in another deal,
As aristocrats ponder, as it's ever so surreal.
We thank society for some of its aristocrats
That believe in equality and are not just fat cats.

(Chorus)
Aristocrats, aristocrats,
Known as little rich brats.
In their corporate land,
They have the upper hand.
Aristocrats, aristocrats, Aristocrats

Ghost Train

(Chorus)
Ghost train, ghost train.
Hitch on a ride on time,
On a horror train of crime.
As passengers board with their pain,
Amidst spirits on a ghost train.
Ghost train, ghost train,
Ghost train.

Verse
(1)
Reflecting through the years
On a never-ending track of fears,
Skeletons in the closet empty out,
River that runs to reality is in drought.
Along a coastline I am guided by a whale,
On this ghost train am I destined to fail.
Repenting in a carriage of life's wrong,
This train may take me to where I belong.
All life's iniquities begin to pile,
Looking for times where I'd smile.
On this ghost train there is no destination

To make amends of an inner observation.
Plagued by dark shadows in a dark tunnel,
Last gasp of life I have is through a funnel.
My reflection shows in these windows of pain,
I am on a journey on this ghost train.

(Chorus)
Ghost train, ghost train,
Hitch on a ride on time,
On a horror train of crime.
As passengers board with their pain,
Amidst spirits of a ghost train.
Ghost train, ghost train,
Ghost train.

Verse

(2)

If I could relax and close my eyes,
Dream of sunshine and blue skies.
My past is like a geographical chase,
Hitching this train to a better place?
All that remains in life is a photograph,
A euphoric recall of when I had a laugh.
Will I ever see the break of a new day?

Like the good old times, how they'd sway.
Is there a time where I once did succeed?
Foot on the throttle as the train picks up speed.
This ghost train may give me a new vision,
To have a chance and make a decision.
All the clubs have been closed down,
This was once the bright spark of town,
What I can do on this ghost train
Is look inside of my cryptic brain.

(Chorus)
Ghost train, ghost train.
Hitch on a ride on time,
On a horror train of crime.
As passengers board with their pain
Amidst spirits of a ghost train.
Ghost train, ghost train,
Ghost train.

Verse
(3)
On board are no Scoobie snacks,
I cannot unwind and relax.
Beams of light shine from outer space,

Am I gone – vanished without a trace?
This ghost train can exceed to time travel,
I'll still have to face the debris to unravel.
As the fog lifts, I am but a ghost.
I was laid to rest down by the west coast.
I move on, I will have learned about history,
Where I'll be tomorrow is a mystery.
On this ghost train is made of evil and good,
I survive the journey in a brotherhood.
For my life I lived in success and in ruin,
A revelation is I am part of a spiritual platoon.
Take me from this entity and ease my pain,
As I am a passenger on this ghost train.

(Chorus)
Ghost train, ghost train.
Hitch on a ride on time,
On a horror train of crime.
As passengers board with their pain,
Amidst spirits of a ghost train.
Ghost train, ghost train,
Ghost train.
Ghost riders of the night,
On a ghost train in full flight.

Hope to be back soon,
From the dark side of the moon.

Ghost train, ghost train,
Oh, ghost train.

Streetwise

(Chorus)

To survive in this darkened town,

As they come to shoot us down.

It's not a game, and there is no prize,

To stay afloat we gotta be streetwise.

Streetwise, streetwise,

We will never say goodbyes,

When we're streetwise.

Streetwise.

Verse

(1)

In this life we have played fools,

Talking from the other side of schools.

Learning the lingo is how it began,

Were we mice or were we men?

Something in our psyche must change,

For our distorted thinking to rearrange.

Streetwise is like the same as being noble,

We could reach the top and even go global.

To know when to talk and turn the other cheek,

Knowledge on the streets has its own critique.

Through the mist we will see the blue skies,
If we're on the ball and become streetwise.
People of faith say light will overcome the dark,
Streetwise we will play oppositions off the park.
To put a bet on surviving and pull out the plugs,
Streetwise you will try, give up drink and drugs.

(Chorus)
To survive in this darkened town,
As they come to shoot us down.
It's not a game and there is no prize,
To stay afloat we gotta be streetwise.
Streetwise, streetwise.
We will never say goodbyes,
When we're streetwise,
Streetwise.

Verse
(2)
On the dark roads we need tunnel vision,
Streetwise is like perfection and precision.
If we come to be in front of a court of law,
It's simple to say who gets the shortest straw.
By keeping our own side of the street clean,

May stop us falling into a chilling movie scene.
If we're on a wrong side of a runaway track,
what's ahead, ask someone who is on the way back.
Just one chance to be a shrewd millionaire,
Live life to fullest, that mistakes we make are rare.
Listening to music as we reach out to hold ecstasy,
If we're streetwise we can live, happy and free.
There are no certificates, degrees or any tests.
Expression of street life dignity and life's quests.
Being streetwise could be never to close the door,
If you're down on your luck and don't know the score.

(Chorus)
To survive in this darkened town,
As they come to shoot us down.
It's not a game and there is no prize,
To stay afloat we gotta be streetwise.
Streetwise, streetwise.
We will never say goodbyes,
When we're streetwise.
Streetwise.

Verse

(3)

If we're lonely, without a friend,
Streetwise may see us to the end.
Simply being as clever as a fox,
Through life's hard-fought knocks.
In this life we need hope and faith,
No one knows their destiny's date.
In society there is low-self-esteem,
When we can't get it right on our team.
In our best when we're boxing so clever,
To be wise, to know nothing lasts forever.
To be at the top we don't need skill and flair,
Wish someone well or say a little prayer.
Climb the mountains and scale the walls,
Streetwise until our higher power calls.
There are two sides to every story,
Streetwise is humility, winning and glory.

(Chorus)

To survive this darkened town,
As they come to hunt us down.
It's not a game and there is no prize,
To stay afloat you gotta be streetwise.

Streetwise, streetwise,
We will never say goodbyes,
When were streetwise.
Streetwise, streetwise,
Streetwise,
Yeah

A Dark Cloud Appears

Verse

(1)

As the sunshine's on my glowing skin,

People say you look great, fresh and thin.

I'd say I've been keeping on top of my game,

Dealing with life's hard knocks and years of shame.

A distance voice says "you coming for a few beers?"

In an instance of doubt a dark cloud appears.

"Ah no, I'll give it a miss. It's getting late."

Reeling me in to take the killer bate,

"It can't harm you, we're all going for a drink."

Just one to a bottomless pit I'll sink.

"We're heading into Copper Face Jacks,

Catch up on old times, have a dance, and relax."

The monkey on my back is saying "go for one".

A dark cloud would block out a light that shun.

If I'd like to return to my nightmare,

Lose touch with reality and those who care.

(Chorus+2)

Temptation will prevail on how I think,

To a bottomless pit I'll surely sink.

I can live in reality by facing my fears
As a dark cloud suddenly appears.

Verse
(2)

"Join in the celebrations, it's Christmas Eve."
"No drink, in my higher power I believe."
One day at a time I can live sober and free,
Living a productive, normal life in reality.
"Come to a party," says Billy, Mary and Mac.
"I'll go, but one drink, I'm never coming back."
I will go to this party as I have a choice,
"We insist on enjoying life," says my inner voice.
At the party most people are getting drunk,
I'm starting enjoy myself or will I do a bunk.
Feeling like a squirrel in winter I'll hibernate,
Maybe if I hang around, I might get a date.
Looking at this liquid that comes in fancy jars,
As I gaze in enlightenment at the moon and stars.
It'd take me on a path to oblivion with one drop,
In a vegetative state, no longer the cream of the crop.

(Chorus+2)

Temptation will prevail on how I think,
To a bottomless pit I'll surely sink.

I can live in reality by facing my fears,
As a dark cloud suddenly appears.

Verse

(3)

It's been a stormy, long, winding road,
If I don't want misery and pain, talk and offload.
Feeling captivated like a rabbit in a headlight,
I'm not getting back in the ring. I'll lose the fight.
Like a Jedi I need to be dynamite on life's beam.
I'm only starting to live, being part of a winning team.
I don't want to be a victim in the alcoholic trenches,
Just to surrender to these obsessive, allergic quenches.
I want to be served as a winning ace,
Not to wake up the next morning feeling a disgrace.
A dark cloud appears, beyond are blue skies.
Think, think twice and continue my life of joys.
Remember those who live in misery and despair,
To carry a message of hope, thankful I'm aware.
Calming the stream with a flow of grateful tears,
Let the sunlight shine, as a dark cloud appears.

(Chorus+2)

Temptation will prevail on how I think,
To a bottomless pit I'll surely sink.

I can live in reality by facing my fears,
As a dark cloud suddenly appears.

An Alleyway to Paradise

Verse

(1)

If life's a cinema, you depend on your seat
To get away for a while if you feel beneath.
It may be your only span of attention
To survive from life's suspension.
In your prime you were beautiful and bold,
Thinking paradise was of glory and gold.
As the stars spangled back you rolled the dice,
This entered you to an alleyway to paradise.
In the hot sun listening to rock 'n' roll,
Rolling out the red carpet as you collected the dole.
Living in a fantasy with a distorted perception,
Coming home with no money expecting a
warm reception.
"Where's my dinner I was just out watching the game
One look as their heart flickered of a sorrowful flame.
You couldn't see the hole as you dug deeper
and deeper,
On the platform of destiny which you are the keeper.

(Chorus+2)
In this life is there a hopeful flame?
As I roll another dice in life's game.
Feeling red hot but as cold as ice,
Pathway to an alleyway to paradise.

Verse

(2)

High as a mountain yet lower than a valley,
Living the dream and nightmare in a paradise alley.
A bottle will help you sleep and stay warm,
Drugs will help you escape from the perilous storm.
In this alley there's no light or sound in the dark,
The thunder and lightning are your only living spark.
Who's to say when walking by no one really cares,
Cavemen surviving the wilderness like hungry bears.
To hear sound of seagulls you may know you're alive,
Every day is Christmas day as the homeless charities arrive.
Mortar and sand are the start of a solid and secure foundation,
Building a life from the bottom is sheer devastation.
Raindrops are washing away your lonely blues,
There is hope as others have once walked in your shoes.

Look up at the starlit night and wish upon a star,
To lead to self-discovery of who you really are.

(Chorus+)
In this life is there a hopeful flame?
As I roll another dice in life's game.
Feeling red hot but as cold as ice,
Pathway to an alleyway to paradise.

Verse
(3)
Sometimes desperation can be as white as snow,
A helping hand can be like a green light, take it and go.
In a dark tunnel you see a light as a vision,
Try to make a break for daylight it's your decision.
If the heavens poured every time it felt your shame,
We'd all drown because we've always someone
to blame.
Life is like we're all caught in a constant whirlpool,
Who can tell the difference of a genius than a fool?
To survive a dark alleyway and you gave some advice,
This can be the difference between men and mice.
Do you want to be a slave to the dark shadows that be,
Or walk in the sunlight and finally say you're free.

You are a miracle through your way of faith,
Giving you a key to reality to unlock the gate.
There mustn't be anything more inspiring and nice,
To say you survived a dark alleyway that led
to paradise.

(Chorus+2)
In this life is there a hopeful flame?
As I roll another dice in life's game.
Feeling red hot but as cold as ice,
Pathway to an alleyway to paradise.

Higher Power

(Chorus)
Higher power, power,
Higher power, power.
In my loneliest darkest hour,
A light shine of my higher power.
Losing all self-control,
As a power cleanse my soul.
Higher power, power,
Higher power.

Verse

(1)

Growing up I was a special child,
Losing direction, I became wild.
Wanting to run with wild dogs,
I became as mad as a box of frogs.
My self-respect became less,
Trying to cope with life's stress.
As authority and society put me down,
I became the meanest dog in the town.
My thinking told me I was cool,
And suburban areas I would rule.

A high-flying bird full of drugs,
Evaporated soul under the rugs.
Growing older and standing tall,
To the sound of a crystal waterfall.
Whichever way the wind blows,
Is a direction only a power knows.

(Chorus)
Higher power, power,
Higher power, power.
In my loneliest, darkest hour,
A light shine of my higher power.
Losing all self-control,
As a power cleanse my soul.
Higher power, power,
Higher power.

Verse
(2)
Taking steps on my weary feet,
Worn out shoes on a lonely street.
Who am I what have I got,
Without my dignity I have not.
I've been caught in the rain shower,
Cooling me down is a higher power.

In a warzone but I can't hear a sound,
I was once lost but know I am found.
I am guided along an enchanted way,
Having faith, I can see a better day.
Over a rainbow and beyond the stars,
There is a power healing my scars.
Like the heroics of the magnificent seven,
Angels are protecting me from heaven.
Taking off the mask as life turns sour,
I gain strength from a higher power.

(Chorus)
Higher power, power,
Higher power, power.
In my loneliest, darkest hour,
A light shine of my higher power.
Losing all self-control,
As a power cleanse my soul.
Higher power, power,
Higher power.

Verse
(3)
I am always sitting on the fence,
Without a power I have no defence.

Trusting in a power I can't see, hear, or smell,
Having faith may open the gates of hell.
If I want to get out of this bottomless pit,
I will have to adjust, accept, and admit.
As a human being I have clay feet,
Without a higher power I am in defeat.
I must let go of ego and pride
For my mind to open wide.
At the end of the line, I have a quote,
Is to seek a higher power or get the boat.
As the joy and glow lightens up my face,
It could be a guidance from a sacred place.
Remember in my darkest, loneliest hour,
No way through without my higher power.

(Chorus)
Higher power, power,
Higher power, power.
In my loneliest, dankest hour,
A light shine of my higher power.
Losing all self-control,
As a power cleanse my soul.
Higher power, power.
Higher power.

Until my destiny's date,
In a higher power I have faith.

When the Earth's sour,
I seek a higher power.

Higher power
Higher power.